MARGINAL NOTES FOR THE
NEW TESTAMENT

Helps for Translators Series

Technical Helps:

Old Testament Quotations in the New Testament
Short Bible Reference System
New Testament Index
The Theory and Practice of Translation
Bible Index
Fauna and Flora of the Bible
Manuscript Preparation
Marginal Notes for the Old Testament
Marginal Notes for the New Testament
The Practice of Translating

Handbooks:

A Translator's Handbook on the Book of Joshua
A Translator's Handbook on the Book of Ruth
A Translator's Handbook on the Book of Amos
A Translator's Handbook on the Books of Obadiah and Micah
A Translator's Handbook on the Book of Jonah
A Translator's Handbook on the Gospel of Matthew
A Translator's Handbook on the Gospel of Mark
A Translator's Handbook on the Gospel of Luke
A Translator's Handbook on the Gospel of John
A Translator's Handbook on the Acts of the Apostles
A Translator's Handbook on Paul's Letter to the Romans
A Translator's Handbook on Paul's First Letter to the Corinthians
A Translator's Handbook on Paul's Letter to the Galatians
A Translator's Handbook on Paul's Letter to the Ephesians
A Translator's Handbook on Paul's Letter to the Philippians
A Translator's Handbook on Paul's Letters to the Colossians and to Philemon
A Translator's Handbook on Paul's Letters to the Thessalonians
A Translator's Handbook on the Letter to the Hebrews
A Translator's Handbook on the First Letter from Peter
A Translator's Handbook on the Letters of John

Guides:

A Translator's Guide to Selections from the First Five Books of the Old Testament
A Translator's Guide to Selected Psalms
A Translator's Guide to the Gospel of Matthew
A Translator's Guide to the Gospel of Mark
A Translator's Guide to the Gospel of Luke
A Translator's Guide to Paul's First Letter to the Corinthians
A Translator's Guide to Paul's Second Letter to the Corinthians
A Translator's Guide to Paul's Letters to Timothy and to Titus
A Translator's Guide to the Letters to James, Peter, and Jude
A Translator's Guide to the Revelation to John

HELPS FOR TRANSLATORS

MARGINAL NOTES FOR THE
NEW TESTAMENT

BASED ON THE TEXT OF
TODAY'S ENGLISH VERSION

by
ROBERT G. BRATCHER

UNITED BIBLE SOCIETIES

London, New York,
Stuttgart

Printed in the United States of America

Books in the series of **Helps for Translators** may be ordered from a national Bible Society, or from either of the following centers:

United Bible Societies
European Production Fund
D-7000 Stuttgart 80
Postfach 81 03 40
West Germany

United Bible Societies
1865 Broadway
New York, New York 10023
U.S.A.

ISBN   0-8267-0026-8

ABS-1988-200-1,200-CM-2-08558

PROVIDING MARGINAL NOTES FOR BIBLE TRANSLATIONS

These Marginal Notes are intended to provide the kind of information that will enable the reader to understand more fully the text of the TEV, the Good News Bible. They are offered to translators as typical of what can and should be done in other languages. Since the TEV is the base for these notes, translators may find it necessary to make adjustments for translations in other languages, all of which present unique problems of their own. These Marginal Notes may be classified as follows:

1. Textual: the more important textual variants are listed; besides those already included in the TEV some others have been added.

2. Translational: translational alternatives are given, particularly for words and phrases usually deemed significant; some alternatives are given which do not appear in the TEV. In some cases the wording for both the textual and the translational notes has been changed from what it is in the TEV, in order to conform more closely to the style of the Notes as a whole.

3. Linguistic: play on words, popular etymologies, meaning of technical words and phrases.

4. Cultural: beliefs, customs, rituals, festivals.

5. People: identification and significance.

6. Historical events: identification and significance.

7. Places: identification (where possible) and significance. Location is usually given in terms of distance from Jerusalem (particularly in the Old Testament), on the assumption that most readers know more or less where Jerusalem is; sometimes, however, the distance is given from the location to which the place is related in the narrative. All distances are given in kilometers.

8. Dates: these conform to the Chronological Table in TEV.

9. References: to other passages in the Bible, particularly in the New Testament.

Notes of the first two types have the alternate texts or translations in ordinary print, while the explanation is underlined. Notes that are explanatory or give a definition, as in types 3 to 9, have the word or phrase underlined that is to be discussed, while the explanation is in ordinary print.

Two additional matters:

1. A dictionary style of definition (not a complete sentence) is generally employed.

2. In compiling these Notes I have consistently consulted: Revised Standard Version, Oxford Study Edition; New English Bible, Oxford Study Edition; Bible de Jérusalem (third edition); Traduction Oecuménique de la Bible; and New American Bible.

Robert G. Bratcher

ABBREVIATIONS OF BOOKS OF THE BIBLE

1,2 Chr	1,2 Chronicles	1,2 Kgs	1,2 Kings
Col	Colossians	Lam	Lamentations
1,2 Cor	1,2 Corinthians	Lev	Leviticus
Dan	Daniel	Mal	Malachi
Deut	Deuteronomy	Matt	Matthew
Eccl	Ecclesiastes	Neh	Nehemiah
Eph	Ephesians	Num	Numbers
Est	Esther	Phil	Philippians
Exo	Exodus	Prov	Proverbs
Ezek	Ezekiel	Psa	Psalms
Gal	Galatians	Rev	Revelation
Gen	Genesis	Rom	Romans
Hab	Habbakuk	1,2 Sam	1,2 Samuel
Hag	Haggai	Song	Song of Solomon
Heb	Hebrews	1,2 Thes	1,2 Thessalonians
Hos	Hosea	1,2 Tim	1,2 Timothy
Isa	Isaiah	Zech	Zechariah
Jer	Jeremiah	Zeph	Zephaniah
Josh	Joshua		

MARGINAL NOTES FOR THE NEW TESTAMENT

BASED ON THE TEXT OF

TODAY'S ENGLISH VERSION

MATTHEW

1.3   Perez and Zerah: twin sons of Judah (see Gen 38.27-30).

1.6   Uriah's wife: Bathsheba (see 2 Sam 12.24).

1.11   Exile in Babylon: in 598 B.C., by King Nebuchadnezzar of Babylonia.

1.12   After the exile in Babylon: in 538 B.C. Emperor Cyrus of Persia allowed the Jews to return to their homeland.

1.17   Messiah: the title (the same as Christ) of the promised Savior whose coming was foretold by the Hebrew prophets.

1.18   Engaged: under Jewish law this relationship was legally binding and could be broken only by a formal act of divorce.

1.21   Jesus: this name in Hebrew means "he saves" or "the Lord is savior."

1.22-23 The Lord had said: see Septuagint Isa 7.14.

2.1   Bethlehem: about 8 kilometers south of Jerusalem.
        Judea: one of the provinces into which the land of Israel was then divided.
        Herod: Herod the Great, king of all the land of Israel 37-4 B.C.

2.4   Chief priests: a group composed of the High Priest, former High Priests still living, and the members of important families from which the High Priests were chosen.
        Teachers of the Law: professionals who interpreted the Hebrew Scriptures, particularly the first five books.
        Messiah: see 1.17.

2.5-6   The prophet wrote: see Micah 5.2; 2 Sam 5.2.

2.11   Frankincense: an aromatic incense, used in sacrifices.
        Myrrh: a perfume made from the hardened sap of a tree.

2.15   The Lord had said: see Hos 11.1.

2.16   All the boys: probably no more than thirty.

2.17-18 The prophet Jeremiah had said: see Jer 31.15.

(1)

2.18   Ramah: a town about 8 kilometers north of Jerusalem; it was near this town that Rachel, the wife of Jacob and mother of Joseph and Benjamin, had been buried (see 1 Sam 10.2).

2.22   Archelaus: son of Herod the Great and ruler of Judea, Samaria, and Idumea 4 B.C.--A.D. 6.
         Galilee: the northern province, ruled by Herod Antipas, brother of Archelaus.

2.23   Nazareth: a town about 26 kilometers west of the southern edge of Lake Galilee.
         He will be called a Nazarene: there is no Old Testament passage in this form; "Nazarene" may reflect "Nazirite" (see Judges 13.5-7), or the word "branch" (see Isa 11.1).

3.1   At that time: John began his ministry probably in A.D. 27 (see Luke 3.1-3).
         The desert of Judea: the desolate region on the west side of the Jordan, not far from where it empties into the Dead Sea.

3.2   Kingdom of heaven: the same as Kingdom of God, meaning God's rule over mankind and the world. Sometimes it is spoken of as a present reality, at other times as a future event; in some instances it is equivalent to eternal life with God.
         is near; or has arrived.

3.3   Isaiah...said: see Septuagint Isa 40.3.

3.4   Clothes made of camel's hair: a robe made of a rough cloth woven from camel's hair.
         Belt: a wide band which not only held the garment tight around the waist but also held money and other items in its folds. John's clothes were like those worn by the prophet Elijah (2 Kgs 1.8).

3.7   Pharisees: a Jewish religious party whose members were strict in obeying the Law of Moses and other regulations which had been added to it through the centuries.
         Sadducees: a small Jewish group, composed largely of priests, who based their beliefs primarily on the first five books of the Hebrew Scriptures.

3.11   carry his sandals: a menial task performed by a slave.

3.13   Galilee: see 2.22.

3.16   Some manuscripts omit to him.

3.17   This is my own dear Son, with whom I am pleased: these words reflect such Old Testament passages as Psa 2.7; Gen 22.2; Isa 42.1.
         my own dear Son; or my only Son; or my Son, the Beloved.

4.1   The desert: see 3.1.
         Devil: the ruler of the forces of evil; the name means "the accuser."

(2)

4.4 The scripture says: see Deut 8.3.

4.6 The scripture says: see Psa 91.11-12.

4.7 The scripture also says: see Deut 6.16.
Satan: another name for the Devil; it means "the opponent."

4.10 The scripture says: see Deut 6.13.

4.12 John...in prison: John the Baptist was arrested and imprisoned by order of Herod Antipas (see Matt 14.3-4), ruler of the provinces of Galilee and Perea.

4.13 Zebulun and Naphtali: two tribes of Israel whose territory was west and north of Lake Galilee.

4.14-16 The prophet Isaiah had said: see Isa 9.1-2.

4.15 Gentiles: people who are not Jews.

4.17 Kingdom of heaven: see 3.2.
is near; or has come.

4.18 Lake Galilee: a body of fresh water in the province of Galilee, some 21 kilometers long and 13 kilometers wide at its widest.
Net: a circular casting net which was looped over the arm and thrown into the water.

4.21 getting their nets ready; or mending their nets.

4.23 Teaching: during the synagogue service anyone, ordained or not, could be asked to instruct the people in the explanation and application of the Hebrew Scriptures.
Synagogues: the public meeting houses where Jews gathered on the Sabbath for worship.
Kingdom: see 3.2.

4.24 Syria: the land of Israel was then part of the Roman province of Syria.
Demons: evil spiritual beings, also called evil spirits or unclean spirits. They were regarded as being able to dominate people, and they were called "unclean" because they caused certain bodily disorders or actions which made people ritually defiled and thus prevented them from taking part in public worship until their defilement had been removed.

4.25 The Ten Towns: a group of Gentile towns mostly on the southeast side of Lake Galilee.
Judea: see 2.1.
Other side: the east side.

5.3 Kingdom of heaven: see 3.2.

5.11   evil lies; some manuscripts have evil things.

5.12   Prophets: God's messengers who proclaimed his message to the people of Israel.

5.15   Lamp: an oil-burning wick lamp, the wick lying in a shallow clay bowl filled with olive oil.
Everyone in the house: the home of most people of that time was a small one-room house.

5.17   Law of Moses: the first five books of the Hebrew Scriptures.
The prophets: the second division of the Hebrew Scriptures. "The Law and the Prophets" was often used to refer to the whole Hebrew Bible.

5.18   the end of all things; or all its teachings come true.

5.19   Kingdom of heaven: see 3.2.

5.20   Teachers of the Law: see 2.4.
Pharisees: see 3.7.

5.21   People were told: see Exo 20.13.

5.22   is angry; some manuscripts add without cause.
Brother: here a member of the same religious group.
Council: the supreme religious court of the Jews, composed of about seventy leaders and presided over by the High Priest.

5.27   It was said: see Exo 20.14.

5.31   It was also said: see Deut 24.1.

5.32   Some manuscripts omit and the man who marries her commits adultery also.

5.33   People were told: see Lev 19.12; Num 30.2; Deut 23.21.

5.37   Evil One: another name for the Devil (see 4.1).

5.38   It was said: see Exo 21.24.

5.40   Shirt: a short-sleeved knee-length garment that was worn next to the body.

5.41   One of the occupation troops: the country was occupied by Roman troops.

5.43   It was said: see Lev 19.18; the words "hate your enemies" are not part of the Old Testament passage.

5.46   Tax collectors: Jews who collected taxes for the Roman government on goods or produce taken in or out of the towns. They were despised by their fellow-Jews, especially the religious leaders, for their failure to keep certain religious rules.

6.4   Some manuscripts add publicly.

6.6   Some manuscripts add publicly.

6.10   Kingdom: see 3.2.

6.11   we need; or for today; or for tomorrow.

6.13   Evil One: see 5.37.
       Some manuscripts add For yours is the kingdom, and the power, and the glory forever. Amen.

6.16   Fast: to abstain temporarily from food as a religious duty.

6.18   Some manuscripts add publicly.

6.19   Moths and rust: much of the wealth of that time consisted of expensive garments and rugs, and metal wares.

6.27   live a bit longer; or grow a bit taller.

6.29   King Solomon: in his time he was the richest of all kings (see 1 Kgs 10.23).

6.33   Kingdom of God: see 3.2.

7.3   Brother: see 5.22.

7.12   Law of Moses and...the prophets: see 5.17.

7.21   Kingdom of heaven: see 3.2; here it refers to heaven, the final abode of God's people.

7.22   Drove out many demons: see 4.24.

7.29   Teachers of the Law: see 2.4.
       Instead, he taught with authority: in contrast with the teachers of the Law, who for their authority quoted the great Jewish teachers of the past.

8.2   Dreaded skin disease: traditionally taken to be leprosy, but probably the biblical term included other skin diseases as well (see Lev 13.1-46; 14.1-32).
       Make me clean: this disease was considered to make a person ritually unclean.

8.3   Touched: all physical contact with a person suffering from this disease was to be avoided.

8.4   The priest: either a local priest or one in the Temple in Jerusalem.

(5)

The sacrifice that Moses ordered: see Lev 14.1-32.

8.5   Capernaum: a town on the northwest shore of Lake Galilee.
Roman officer: probably the army officer in charge of the
local Roman occupation troops (see 5.41).

8.11   The feast in the Kingdom of heaven: see 7.21.

8.12   Those who should be in the Kingdom: the people of Israel.

8.16   demons...evil spirits: see 4.24.

8.17   Isaiah had said: see Isa 53.4.

8.18   The other side: the east side of Lake Galilee (see 4.18).

8.19   Teacher of the Law: see 2.4.

8.20   Son of Man: a title of dignity, used only of Jesus in the New
Testament. In some passages it refers to the future coming of
Jesus in power.

8.21   Bury my father: an expression that probably means "take care of
my father until he dies."

8.28   Gadara; some manuscripts have Gergesa; others have Gerasa (see
Mark 5.1).
Gadara: a Gentile town some 18 kilometers southeast of Lake
Galilee.
The other side: the east side.
Demons: see 4.24.

8.29   What do you want with us?: an idiomatic phrase (see Septuagint
Judges 11.12; 2 Sam 16.10; 1 Kgs 17.18) expressing hostility.
The right time: the final Day of Judgment.

8.33   The town: Gadara (see verse 28).

9.1   Went back across: to the west side.
His own town: Capernaum (see 4.13).

9.2   Faith: the faith of the people, and probably of the sick man
himself, in Jesus' power to heal.
My son: an expression of endearment.

9.3   Teachers of the Law: see 2.4.

9.6   Son of Man: see 8.20.

9.9   Tax collector: see 5.46.

9.10   in Matthew's house; or in his (that is, Jesus') house.
Other outcasts: people who like the tax collectors were despised

(6)

by the religious leaders because of their refusal to obey all the religious rules, especially those which prohibited the eating of certain foods and associating with Gentiles.

9.11   Pharisees: see 3.7.

9.13   The scripture that says: see Hos 6.6.
respectable; or good.

9.14   Pharisees: see 3.7.
Fast: see 6.16.
Some manuscripts omit often.

9.15   guests at a wedding party; or a bridegroom's attendants.

9.18   Official: identified as the presiding officer of the local synagogue in Mark 5.22.

9.20   Severe bleeding: due to menstrual disorder.
The edge: the tassels which pious Jews wore on the edges of their cloaks as a sign of devotion to God (see Num 15.37-41; Matt 23.5).

9.22   My daughter: an expression of endearment (see 9.2).

9.27   Son of David: a title the Jews used of the promised Savior as the descendant and successor of King David.

9.32   Demon: see 4.24.

9.34   Some manuscripts omit this verse.
The chief of demons: the Devil (see 4.1).

9.35   Synagogues: see 4.23.
Kingdom: see 3.2.

10.1   Drive out evil spirits: see 4.24.

10.2   Apostles: men who were commissioned to speak and act with the authority of the one who sent them.

10.4   The Patriot: so called perhaps because he was, or had been, a member of a nationalist party which advocated the overthrow of the Roman authority by force if necessary.

10.5   Gentile: see 4.15.

10.6   Samaritan: a native of Samaria, the province between Judea and Galilee. There was much hostility between Jews and Samaritans because of differences in race, customs, politics, and religion.

10.7   Kingdom of heaven: see 3.2.
is near; or has arrived.

10.8   Dreaded skin diseases: see 8.2.
          Drive out demons: see 4.24.

10.9   Pockets: see 3.4.

10.10   Shirt: see 5.40.

10.12   Peace be with you: the customary greeting.

10.14   Shake the dust off your feet: a sign of complete rejection.

10.15   Sodom and Gomorrah: two cities near the Dead Sea which God destroyed by fire because of the great wickedness of the people (see Gen 19.24-28).

10.17   Synagogues: see 4.23.

10.23   Son of Man: see 8.20.

10.25   Beelzebul: the name given the Devil as the ruler of the evil spirits; it is probably related to the name of the Philistine god Baalzebub (see 2 Kgs 1.2-3).

11.2   John the Baptist...in prison: see 14.3-4.
          Christ; or the Messiah.
          some; some manuscripts have two.

11.5   Dreaded skin diseases: see 8.2.

11.10   The scripture says: see Mal 3.1; "ahead of you" may be from Exo 23.20.

11.11   Kingdom of heaven: see 3.2.

11.12   has suffered violent attacks; or has been coming violently.

11.13   All the prophets and the Law of Moses: see 5.17.

11.14   Elijah, whose coming was predicted: see Mal 4.5-6.

11.18   Fasted: see 6.16.
          Demon: see 4.24.

11.19   Son of Man: see 8.20.
          Tax collectors: see 5.46.
          Outcasts: see 9.10.

11.21   Tyre and Sidon: Gentile cities on the Mediterranean coast, north of Galilee.

11.23   Did you...heaven? You will...hell: see Isa 14.13,15.
          Sodom: see 10.15.

11.29   Yoke: a figure of the instructions that a teacher passes on to his pupils. The Jewish teachers spoke of the Law of Moses as a yoke.

12.1   Sabbath: the seventh day of the Jewish week, the holy day on which no work was allowed.

12.2   Pharisees: see 3.7.
         Our Law: the Hebrew Scriptures, especially the first five books.
         To do this: reaping, which was forbidden on the Sabbath (see Exo 34.21).

12.3-4   What David did: see 1 Sam 21.1-6.

12.4   The house of God: the Tent of the Lord's presence (see Exo 36. 8-38).
         The bread offered to God: see Lev 24.5-9.

12.5   The priests...break the Sabbath law: by doing the work needed for offering sacrifices (see Num 28.9-10).

12.7   The scripture says: see Hos 6.6.

12.8   Son of Man: see 8.20.

12.9   Synagogue: see 4.23.

12.10   Our Law: see 12.2.
         Sabbath: see 12.1.

12.14   Pharisees: see 3.7.

12.17-21 God had said: see Isa 42.1-3; for verse 21 see Septuagint Isa 42.4.

12.20   A bent reed...a flickering lamp: figures of people who are helpless and weak.

12.22   Demon: see 4.24.

12.23   Son of David: see 9.27.

12.24   Beelzebul: see 10.25.

12.26   Satan: see 4.7.

12.28   Kingdom of God: see 3.2.

12.31   evil thing they say; or evil thing they say against God.

12.32   Son of Man: see 8.20.

12.36   Teachers of the Law: see 2.4.
         Pharisees: see 3.7.

(9)

12.40   Jonah: see Jonah 1.17.
       Son of Man: see 8.20.

12.42   The Queen of Sheba: see 1 Kgs 10.1-10.

12.43   Evil spirit: see 4.24.
       Dry country: the desert was thought to be the place where evil
spirits liked to live.

12.47   Some manuscripts omit this verse.

13.1   Lakeside: Lake Galilee (see 4.18).

13.3   Parables: stories using everyday matters to teach spiritual
lessons.

13.10   Parables: see 13.3.

13.11   Kingdom of heaven: see 3.2.

13.14-15 The prophecy of Isaiah: see Septuagint Isa 6.9-10.

13.17   Prophets: see 5.12.

13.19   Evil One: see 5.37.

13.32   Plants: garden plants or shrubs.

13.35   The prophet: in the Old Testament Asaph is named as the author
of Psalm 78.
       the prophet; some manuscripts have the prophet Isaiah.
       Had said: see Septuagint Psalm 78.2.

13.37   Son of Man: see 8.20.

13.38   Kingdom: see 3.2.

13.39   Evil One: see 5.37.

13.47   Net: a large net which was pulled through the water in a
semi-circle.

13.52   Teacher of the Law: see 2.4.

13.54   His home town: Nazareth.
       Taught in the synagogue: see 4.23.

13.57   Prophet: see 5.12.

14.1   Herod: Herod Antipas, ruler of the provinces of Galilee and
Perea 4 B.C.--A.D. 39.

14.3   Philip: Herod's half-brother who lived in Rome.

14.13 In a boat: on Lake Galilee.

14.22 The other side: the west side.

14.30 Some manuscripts omit strong.

14.34 Gennesaret: a fertile plain on the northwest shore of Lake Galilee.

14.36 The edge: see 9.20.

15.1 Pharisees: see 3.7.
Teachers of the Law: see 2.4.

15.4 God said: see Exo 20.12; 21.17.

15.6 his father; some manuscripts have his father or mother.

15.7-9 Isaiah...prophesied: this quotation from Isa 29.13 follows the Septuagint but is not identical with it.

15.12 Pharisees: see 3.7.

15.14 Some manuscripts omit of the blind.

15.21 Tyre and Sidon: see 11.21.

15.22 Canaanite: a Gentile, born in that part of the Roman province of Syria (see Mark 7.26).
Son of David: see 9.27.
Demon: see 4.24.

15.29 Lake Galilee: see 4.18.

15.39 Magadan; some manuscripts have Magdala.
Magadan: a place of uncertain location on the west shore of Lake Galilee.

16.1 Pharisees and Sadducees: see 3.7.

16.3 Some manuscripts omit the words of Jesus in verses 2-3.

16.4 The miracle of Jonah: see 12.39-40.

16.5 The other side: the east side.

16.6 Pharisees and Sadducees: see 3.7.

16.13 Caesarea Philippi: some 40 kilometers north of Lake Galilee.
Son of Man: see 8.20.

16.14 Elijah: a Hebrew prophet the Jews expected to return and prepare the way for the Messiah (see Mal 4.5-6).

16.15   Prophets: see 5.12.

16.16   Messiah: see 1.17.

16.18   Rock...rock foundation: there is a play on the Greek words petros "rock" and petra "rock foundation." Jesus says to Simon, "You are petros and on this petra I will build my church."

16.19   Kingdom of heaven: see 3.2.

16.21   Jesus; some manuscripts add Christ.
Elders: respected Jewish religious leaders, some of whom were members of the Supreme Council.
Chief priests, and the teachers of the Law: see 2.4.

16.23   Satan: see 4.7.

16.27   Son of Man: see 8.20.

17.5   This is my own dear Son, with whom I am pleased: see 3.17.
my own dear Son; or my only Son; or my Son, the Beloved.

17.9   Son of Man: see 8.20.

17.10   Teachers of the Law: see 2.4.
Elijah has to come first: see 16.14.

17.18   Demon: see 4.24.

17.20   enough faith; some manuscripts have any faith.
Some manuscripts add verse 21: But only prayer and fasting can drive this kind out; nothing else can (see Mark 9.29).

17.23   Son of Man: see 8.20.

17.24   Capernaum: see 8.5.
Temple tax: every adult male Jew had to pay annually for support of the Temple an amount equivalent to two days' wages of a rural worker.

17.27   The lake: Lake Galilee.

18.1   Kingdom of heaven: see 3.2.

18.10   Their angels in heaven: this seems to refer to the belief that each person had an angel to watch over him.
Some manuscripts add verse 11: For the Son of Man came to save the lost (see Luke 19.10).

18.14   you; some manuscripts have my.

18.15   Brother: see 5.22.
Some manuscripts omit against you.

18.16   The scripture says: see Deut 19.15.

18.17   Tax collector: see 5.46.

18.21   Brother: see 5.22.

18.22   seventy times seven; or seventy-seven times.

18.23   Kingdom of heaven: see 3.2.

19.1   Galilee: see 2.22.
         Judea: see 2.1.
         The other side: the east side.

19.3   Pharisees: see 3.7.
         Our Law: see 12.2.

19.4   The scripture that says: see Gen 1.27.

19.5   God said: see Gen 2.24.

19.7   Moses give the law: see Deut 24.1.

19.9   Some manuscripts add and the man who marries the divorced woman
         commits adultery also (see Matt 5.32).

19.12   Kingdom of heaven: see 3.2.

19.18-19 Commandments: see Exo 20.12-16; Lev 19.18.

19.23   Kingdom of heaven: see 3.2.

19.28   Son of Man: see 8.20.

19.29   Some manuscripts add or wife (see Luke 18.29).

20.1   Kingdom of heaven: see 3.2.

20.15   with my own money; or on my own property.

20.18   Son of Man: see 8.20.
         Chief priests and the teachers of the Law: see 2.4.

20.19   The Gentiles: the Roman authorities.

20.20   Two sons: the apostles James and John (see Mark 10.35).

20.28   Son of Man: see 8.20.

20.29   Jericho: a city west of the Jordan, some 24 kilometers northeast
         of Jerusalem.

20.30   Son of David: see 9.27.

(13)

21.1   Mount of Olives: just to the east of Jerusalem, across Kidron
Valley.

21.3   The Master; or Their owner.
'The Master...at once."; or 'The Master needs them, but he will
return them at once.'"

21.4-5   The prophet had said: see Isa 62.11; Zech 9.9.

21.11   Prophet: see 5.12.

21.12   Who were buying and selling: for the convenience of worshipers
who came from distant places, animals fit for being offered in
sacrifice were sold in the Temple area.
Moneychangers: men who exchanged foreign currency into the
proper coin for paying the Temple tax and for buying animals to be
offered as sacrifice.

21.13   God said: see Isa 56.7.
Hideout for thieves: see Jer 7.11.

21.15   Chief priests and the teachers of the Law: see 2.4.
David's Son: see 9.27.

21.16   This scripture: see Septuagint Psa 8.2.

21.17   Bethany: a town about 3 kilometers east of Jerusalem.

21.23   Chief priests: see 2.4.
Elders: see 16.21.

21.26   Prophet: see 5.12.

21.31   Tax collectors: see 5.46.
Kingdom of God: see 3.2.

21.33   Parable: see 13.3.

21.42   The Scriptures say: see Psa 118.22-23.

21.43   Kingdom of God: see 3.2.
Some manuscripts add verse 44: Whoever falls on this stone will
be cut to pieces; and if the stone falls on someone, it will crush
him to dust (see Luke 20.18).

21.45   Chief priests: see 2.4.
Pharisees: see 3.7.

21.46   Prophet: see 5.12.

22.1   Parables: see 13.3.

22.2   Kingdom of heaven: see 3.2.

(14)

22.15   Pharisees: see 3.7.

22.16   Herod's party: a Jewish political party which favored one of the descendants of Herod the Great as ruler instead of the Roman governor.

22.17   Our Law: see 12.2.
Roman Emperor: at that time Tiberius, who ruled A.D. 14-37.

22.19   The coin: a Roman silver coin called denarius.

22.23   Sadducees: see 3.7.

22.24   Moses said: see Deut 25.5-6.

22.29   The Scriptures: the Hebrew Bible.

22.31-32 He said: see Exo 3.6.

22.34   Pharisees...Sadducees: see 3.7.

22.35   Some manuscripts omit a teacher of the Law.

22.36-37 The greatest commandment: see Deut 6.5; instead of "your mind," the Old Testament passage has "your strength."

22.39   The second most important commandment: see Lev 19.18.

22.40   Law of Moses and...the prophets: see 5.17.

22.41   Pharisees: see 3.7.
Messiah: see 1.17.

22.43-44 David said: see Psa 110.1.

22.44   Right side: the place of honor and authority.
Under your feet: a figure of defeat and humiliation.

23.2   Teachers of the Law: see 2.4.
Pharisees: see 3.7.

23.5   Straps with scripture verses on them: small leather cases, tied around the forehead and left arm, in which were placed important passages from the Hebrew Scriptures, in literal obedience to Deut 6.8; 11.18.
Tassels: these tassels, one on each of the four corners of the cloak, were worn as a sign of devotion to God (see Num 15.37-41).

23.6   Synagogues: see 4.23.

23.10   Messiah: see 1.17.

23.13   Teachers of the Law: see 2.4.

(15)

Pharisees: see 3.7.
Kingdom of heaven: see 3.2.
Some manuscripts add verse 14: How terrible for you, teachers
of the Law and Pharisees! You hypocrites! You take advantage of
widows and rob them of their homes, and then make a show of saying
long prayers! Because of this your punishment will be all the
worse! (see Mark 12.40).

23.29   Prophets: see 5.12.

23.34   Synagogues: see 4.23.

23.35   Zechariah son of Berechiah: the reference is to the murder of
Zechariah son of Jehoiada the priest (see 2 Chr 24.20-22), the
last murder reported in the Hebrew Scriptures (2 Chronicles is
the last in the arrangement of books in the Hebrew Bible), as
Abel's was the first (Gen 4.8). Zechariah son of Berechiah was
another man (Zech 1.1).

24.3   Mount of Olives: see 21.1

24.5   Messiah: see 1.17.

24.14   Kingdom: see 3.2.

24.15   The Awful Horror: the expression, as translated into Greek by
the Septuagint of Dan 11.31; 12.11, referring to the heathen altar
set up in the Temple by the Syrian king Antiochus Epiphanes in 167
B.C.; here a pagan altar or idol is meant.
        Reader: the person who read the passage aloud to the assembled
congregation.

24.16   Judea: see 2.1.

24.17   Roof: flat, reached by outside steps, a place where people
would go at the end of the day for rest and relaxation.

24.20   Sabbath: not only was work not permitted (see 12.1), but it was
also forbidden to travel more than half a mile on that day.

24.24   Prophets: see 5.12.

24.27   Son of Man: see 8.20.

24.29   The powers in space: the stars and planets, which were believed
to be controlled by spiritual powers.

24.30   Son of Man: see 8.20.

24.33   the time is near, ready to begin; or he is near, ready to come.

24.36   Some manuscripts omit nor the Son.

24.38-39 The flood: see Gen 7.6-23.

24.51 cut him in pieces; or throw him out.

25.1 Kingdom of heaven: see 3.2.
Lamps: see 5.15.
Some manuscripts add and the bride.

25.31 Son of Man: see 8.20.

25.40 Brothers: see 5.22.

25.41 Devil: see 4.1.

26.2 Passover: a festival held on the 14th day of Nisan (around
April 1), which celebrated the deliverance of the ancient Hebrews
from their slavery in Egypt.
Son of Man: see 8.20.

26.3 Chief priests: see 2.4.
Elders: see 16.21.
High Priest: the priest who occupied the highest office in the
Jewish priestly system and who was president of the Supreme Council
of the Jews.

26.6 Bethany: see 21.17.
Dreaded skin disease: see 8.2.

26.7 Alabaster: a soft stone of light, creamy color, from which vases
and jars were made.

26.14 Chief priests: see 2.4.

26.17 Unleavened Bread: the festival held Nisan 15-22 (around the
first part of April), which celebrated the deliverance of the
ancient Hebrews from their slavery in Egypt. Its name came from
the practice of not using leaven (yeast) in making bread during
that week.
Passover: see 26.2.

26.18 The city: Jerusalem.

26.23 The dish: the dish which held the sauces into which the bread
was dipped.

26.24 Son of Man: see 8.20.
Scriptures: see 22.29.

26.25 So you say; or Yes, it is as you say.

26.28 Blood, which seals the covenant: God's covenant with the people
of Israel was sealed by blood of the sacrificed animals being
sprinkled on the people (Exo 24.7-8).

(17)

covenant; <u>some manuscripts have</u> new covenant (<u>see Luke 22.20</u>).

26.29   <u>Kingdom</u>: see 3.2.

26.30   <u>A hymn</u>: Psalms 115-118 were customarily sung at the end of the Passover meal.
<u>Mount of Olives</u>: see 21.1.

26.31   <u>The scripture says</u>: see Zech 13.7; there God commands his sword to <u>kill the shepherd</u>.

26.36   <u>Gethsemane</u>: a garden on the western slope of the Mount of Olives.

26.45   Are you still sleeping and resting? <u>or</u> Keep on sleeping and resting.
<u>Son of Man</u>: see 8.20.

26.47   <u>Chief priests</u>: see 2.4.
<u>Elders</u>: see 16.21.

26.50   Be quick about it, friend!; <u>or</u> Why are you here, friend?
<u>High Priest</u>: see 26.3.

26.54   <u>Scriptures</u>: see 22.29.

26.56   <u>The prophets</u>: see 5.17.

26.57   <u>High Priest</u>: see 26.3.
<u>Teachers of the Law</u>: see 2.4.
<u>Elders</u>: see 16.21.

26.59   <u>Council</u>: see 5.22.

26.63   <u>Messiah</u>: see 1.17.

26.64   So you say; <u>or</u> Yes, it is as you say.
<u>Son of Man</u>: see 8.20.
<u>The right</u> side: see 22.44.

26.65   <u>Tore his clothes</u>: a ritual act expressing outrage and horror.

26.69   <u>Jesus of Galilee</u>: frequently a person was identified by the place he was from; for example, Elijah of Tishbe (1 Kgs 17.1); Joseph of Arimathea (Mark 15.43); Saul of Tarsus (Acts 9.11).

26.71   <u>Jesus of Nazareth</u>: see 26.69.

26.73   <u>The way you speak</u>: Peter's accent showed he was from Galilee.

27.1   <u>Chief priests</u>: see 2.4.
<u>Elders</u>: see 16.21.

27.2   Pilate: Pontius Pilate, Roman governor of Judea, Samaria, and Idumea, A.D. 26-36.

27.6   Our Law: see 12.2.

27.9-10   Jeremiah had said: see Zech 11.12-13; the attribution of the passage to the prophet Jeremiah may be due to the fact that Jeremiah speaks of a potter (18.1-3) and of buying a field (32.6-10).

27.10   used; some manuscripts have I used. (In this case, "They took" in verse 9 would instead be translated "I took.")

27.11   So you say; or Yes, it is as you say.

27.15   Passover: see 26.2.

27.16,17   Jesus Barabbas; many manuscripts have Barabbas.

27.17   Messiah: see 1.17.

27.24   this man; some manuscripts have this innocent man.

27.32   Cyrene: the capital of Libya, a country in North Africa. Cross: here the horizontal beam which the condemned man was forced to carry to the place of execution.

27.34   Bitter substance: probably a drug, to lessen the suffering (see Mark 15.23).

27.35   A few manuscripts add in order to make come true what the prophet had said, "They divided my clothes among themselves and gambled for my robe" (see John 19.24).

27.38   bandits; or insurrectionists.

27.41   Chief priests and the teachers of the Law: see 2.4. Elders: see 16.21.

27.45   country; or world.

27.46   Eli, Eli, lema sabachthani?: a transliteration of the Hebrew form of "my God, my God" and the Aramaic form of "why did you abandon me?" See Psa 22.1.

27.47   Elijah: in Hebrew "Elijah" and "Eli" sound somewhat alike.

27.49   Some manuscripts add Another man took a spear and plunged it into Jesus' side, and water and blood poured out (see John 19.34).

27.51   Curtain: the large curtain separating the Holy Place from the Most Holy Place.

27.53 Holy City: Jerusalem.

27.56 Magdalene: from Magdala, a town on the west side of Lake Galilee.

27.57 Evening: before sunset, when the Sabbath would begin.
Arimathea: a town some 35 kilometers northwest of Jerusalem.

27.61 Magdalene: see 27.56.
The other Mary: see 27.56.

27.62 Sabbath: see 12.1.
Chief priests: see 2.4.
Pharisees: see 3.7.

27.65 Take; or You have.

28.1 Magdalene: see 27.56.
The other Mary: see 27.56.

28.10 Brothers: see 5.22.

28.11 The city: Jerusalem.
Chief priests: see 2.4.

28.12 Elders: see 16.21.

28.14 Governor: Pilate (see 27.2).

28.15 This very day: the time of the writing of this Gospel.

28.17 some of them; or they.

MARK

1.1 Verse 1 may be connected to verse 2 "The Good News...began [2]as written by the prophet Isaiah"; or it may be connected with verse 4 (verses 2-3 being treated parenthetically). Some manuscripts omit the Son of God.

1.2 Isaiah had written: see Mal 3.1; "ahead of you" may be from Exo 23.20.

1.3 Someone is shouting: see Septuagint Isa 40.3; "for him" replaces "for our God" in Isa.

1.4 Some manuscripts have John the Baptist appeared in the desert, preaching; others have John appeared, who baptized and preached.
Appeared: John began his ministry probably in A.D. 27 (see Luke 3.1-3).
The desert: the desolate region on the west side of the Jordan, not far from where it empties into the Dead Sea.

1.5   Judea: one of the provinces into which the land of Israel was then divided.

1.6   Clothes made of camel's hair: a robe made of a rough cloth woven from camel's hair.
Belt: a wide band which not only held the garment tight around the waist but also held money and other items in its folds. John's clothes were like those worn by the prophet Elijah (2 Kgs 1.8).

1.7   Bend down and untie his sandals: a menial task performed by a servant.

1.9   Nazareth: a town about 26 kilometers west of the southern edge of Lake Galilee.
Galilee: the province in the north, governed by Herod Antipas, son of Herod the Great.

1.10   coming down on him; or coming down to enter him.

1.11   You are my own dear Son. I am pleased with you: these words reflect such Old Testament passages as Psa 2.7; Gen 22.2; Isa 42.1.
my own dear Son; or my only Son; or my Son, the Beloved.

1.12   Desert: see 1.4.

1.13   Satan: the ruler of the forces of evil; the name means "the opponent."
Wild animals: such as hyenas, jackals, foxes, gazelles.

1.14   John...in prison: John the Baptist was arrested by order of Herod Antipas (see Mark 6.17-18), governor of the provinces of Galilee and Perea.

1.15   The Kingdom of God: God's rule over mankind and the world.
is near; or has arrived.

1.16   Lake Galilee: a body of fresh water in the province of Galilee, some 21 kilometers long and 13 kilometers wide at its widest.
Net: a circular casting net which was looped over the arm and thrown out into the water.

1.19   getting their nets ready; or mending their nets.

1.20   Hired men: men who were hired to help with the fishing.

1.21   Capernaum: a town on the northwest shore of Lake Galilee.
Sabbath: the seventh day of the Jewish week, the holy day on which no work was allowed.
Synagogue: the public meeting house where Jews gathered on the Sabbath for worship.
Teach: during the synagogue service anyone, ordained or not, could be asked to instruct the people in the explanation and application of the Scriptures.

1.22   Teachers of the Law: professionals who interpreted the Old
Testament, particularly the first five books. Their authority lay
in large measure in their ability to quote the opinions of famous
teachers of the past.

1.23   Evil spirit: a spirit which was regarded as being able to
dominate people. It was called "unclean" because it caused certain
bodily disorders or actions which made people ritually defiled and
thus prevented them from taking part in public worship until their
defilement had been removed.

1.24   Us: either all evil spirits as a class, or the numerous spirits
which had possessed the man.
        Jesus of Nazareth: frequently a person was identified by the
place he was from; for example, Elijah of Tishbe (1 Kgs 17.1);
Joseph of Arimathea (Mark 15.43); Saul of Tarsus (Acts 9.11).
        God's holy messenger; or God's Holy One. Probably a title for
the Messiah.

1.27   Is it some kind...give orders; or It is a new teaching with
authority. He gives orders; or It is a new teaching. This man has
authority. He gives orders.

1.28   Galilee: see 1.9.

1.29   Synagogue: see 1.21.

1.32   After the sun had set and evening had come: the Jewish day
ended at sunset, and now that the Sabbath (verse 21) was over,
people were allowed to engage in normal activities.
        Demons: the same as evil spirits (see 1.23).

1.33   The town: Capernaum (verse 21).

1.34   Drove out: by ordering them to leave the persons they possessed
(see 1.25-26).
        Who he was: they knew he was the Messiah (see 1.24).

1.39   Galilee: see 1.9.
        Synagogues: see 1.21.
        Driving out demons: see 1.23,34.

1.40   A dreaded skin disease: traditionally taken to be leprosy, but
probably the biblical term included other skin diseases as well
(see Lev 13.1-46; 14.1-32).
        Make me clean: the disease was considered to make a person
ritually impure.

1.41   pity; some manuscripts have anger.
        Touched: all physical contact was to be avoided with a person
suffering from this disease.

1.44   The priest: either a local priest or one in the Temple in
Jerusalem.

The sacrifice that Moses ordered: see Lev 14.1-32.

2.1   At home: either in Simon Peter's house (1.29) or else his own house (see 2.15).

2.4   The roof: outside steps led up to the flat roof, which was usually made of wood and branches, covered over with packed earth, so that it was not difficult to dig a hole through it.
Mat: usually a mattress of coarse cloth.

2.5   Their faith: the faith of the four men, and probably of the sick man himself, in Jesus' power to heal.
My son: an expression of endearment.

2.6   Teachers of the Law: see 1.22.

2.10   Son of Man: a title of dignity, used only of Jesus in the New Testament.

2.13   Lake Galilee: see 1.16.

2.14   Tax collector: one who collected taxes for the Roman government on goods or produce taken in or out of the town.
Levi: called Matthew in Matt 9.9.

2.15   in Levi's house; or in Jesus' house (in Capernaum: see 2.1).
Other outcasts: people who like the tax collectors were despised by the religious leaders because of their refusal to obey all the religious rules, especially those which prohibited eating certain foods and associating with Gentiles.

2.16   Teachers of the Law: see 1.22.
Pharisees: a Jewish religious party whose members were strict in obeying the Law of Moses and other regulations which had been added to it through the centuries.

2.17   respectable; or good.

2.18   Pharisees: see 2.16.
Fasting: abstaining temporarily from food as a religious duty.

2.19   guests at a wedding party; or a bridegroom's attendants.

2.22   Some manuscripts omit Instead, new wine must be poured into fresh wineskins.

2.23   Sabbath: see 1.21.

2.24   Pharisees: see 2.16.
Our Law: the Hebrew Scriptures, especially the first five books.
To do that: reaping, which was forbidden on the Sabbath (see Exo 34.21).

(23)

2.25-26   <u>What David did</u>: see 1 Sam 21.1-6.

2.26   <u>The house of God</u>: the Tent of the Lord's presence (see Exo 36.8-38).
    <u>The bread offered to God</u>: see Lev 24.5-9.
    <u>Abiathar</u>: see 2 Sam 20.25; the priest who gave David the bread was Abiathar's father Ahimelech.
    <u>High Priest</u>: the priest who occupied the highest office in the Jewish priestly system and who was president of the Supreme Council of the Jews.

2.28   <u>Son of Man</u>: see 2.10.

3.1   <u>Synagogue</u>: see 1.21.

3.2   <u>Sabbath</u>: see 1.21.

3.4   <u>Our Law</u>: see 2.24.

3.6   <u>Pharisees</u>: see 2.16.
    <u>Herod's party</u>: a Jewish political party which favored one of the descendants of Herod the Great as ruler instead of the Roman governor.

3.7   <u>Lake Galilee</u>: see 1.16.
    <u>Galilee</u>: see 1.9.
    <u>Judea</u>: see 1.5.

3.8   <u>Idumea</u>: the southernmost province of the country.
    <u>Tyre and Sidon</u>: Gentile cities on the Mediterranean coast, north of Galilee.

3.11   <u>Evil spirits</u>: see 1.23.

3.12   <u>Who he was</u>: see 1.34.

3.14   <u>Some manuscripts omit</u> whom he named apostles.
    <u>Apostles</u>: men who were commissioned to speak and act with the authority of the one who sent them.

3.15   <u>Drive out demons</u>: see 1.23,34.

3.18   <u>The Patriot</u>: so called perhaps because he was, or had been, a member of a nationalist party which advocated the overthrow of the Roman authority by force if necessary.

3.20   <u>Home</u>: probably in Capernaum (see 2.15).

3.21   <u>His family</u>: his mother, brothers, and sisters (see verses 31-32).
    <u>people</u>; <u>or</u> they.

3.22   <u>Teachers of the Law</u>: see 1.22.
    <u>Beelzebul</u>: the name given the Devil as the ruler of the evil

spirits; the name is probably related to the name of the Philistine god Baalzebub (see 2 Kgs 1.2-3).

3.23   Parables: stories using everyday matters to teach spiritual lessons.
Satan: see 1.13.

3.28   evil things they may say; or evil things they may say against God.

3.32   Some manuscripts omit and sisters.

4.1   Lake Galilee: see 1.16.

4.2   Parables: see 3.23.

4.10   Parables: see 3.23.

4.11   Kingdom of God: see 1.15.

4.12   So that: what follows is a free quotation of Septuagint Isa 6.9-10; "and he would forgive them" replaces the Septuagint "and I would heal them."

4.13   Parable: see 3.23.

4.15   Satan: see 1.13.

4.21   Lamp: an oil-burning wick lamp, the wick lying in a shallow clay bowl filled with olive oil.
Bowl: a large bowl holding about 9 liters, in which grain was kept.

4.26   Kingdom of God: see 1.15.

4.30   Parable: see 3.23.

4.32   Plants: garden plants or shrubs.

4.35   The other side: the east side.

4.38   Pillow: probably a rough cushion ordinarily used by the man rowing.

5.1   Other side: the east side.
Lake Galilee: see 1.16.
Gerasa; some manuscripts have Gadara (see Matt 8.28); others have Gergesa.
Gerasa: a Gentile town, apparently some 60 kilometers southeast of Lake Galilee.

5.2   Evil spirit: see 1.23.

5.9 Mob: the large number of evil spirits is referred to as a legion, which was a unit in the Roman army composed of some 6,000 soldiers. Us: the evil spirits possessing the man.

5.10 That region: of Gerasa (see verse 1).

5.14 The town: Gerasa (see verse 1).

5.20 The Ten Towns: a group of Gentile towns mostly on the southeast side of Lake Galilee, of which Gerasa was one.

5.21 across; some manuscripts add in the boat. The other side: the west side.

5.22 Synagogue: see 1.21.

5.25 Severe bleeding: due to menstrual disorder.

5.25-26 suffered terribly...doctors; or had a severe bleeding for twelve years and had suffered terribly from the treatment of many doctors.

5.34 My daughter: an expression of endearment.

5.36 paid no attention to; or overheard.

5.41 Talitha, koum: a transliteration of the Aramaic words spoken by Jesus.

6.1 His home town: Nazareth.

6.2 Sabbath: see 1.21.
Teach: see 1.21.
Synagogue: see 1.21.

6.3 the carpenter, the son of Mary; some manuscripts have the son of the carpenter and Mary (see Matt 13.55).

6.4 Prophet: a person who proclaims God's message.

6.7 Evil spirits: see 1.23.

6.8 Pockets: see belt in 1.6.

6.9 Shirt: a short-sleeved knee-length garment that was worn next to the body.

6.11 Shake the dust off your feet: a sign of complete rejection.

6.13 Drove out...demons: see 1.23,34.
Rubbed olive oil: a medicinal practice of the time.

6.14 King Herod: Herod Antipas, ruler of Galilee (see 1.14).

some people were saying; some manuscripts have Herod said.

6.15   Elijah: a Hebrew prophet the Jews expected to return and prepare the way for the Messiah (see Mal 4.5-6).
Prophet: see 6.4.

6.17   Philip: Herod's half-brother who lived in Rome.

6.20   became greatly disturbed; some manuscripts have did many things.

6.21   Galilee: see 1.9.

6.22   The daughter of Herodias; some manuscripts have His daughter Herodias.

6.30   Apostles: see 3.14.
Returned: from the trip on which Jesus had sent them (see 6.7-13).

6.32   In a boat: on Lake Galilee.

6.33   who they were; or where they were going.

6.37   Silver coins: a silver coin was the daily wage of a rural worker (see Matt 20.2).

6.40   in groups of a hundred and groups of fifty; or a hundred rows of fifty people each.

6.43   the disciples took up twelve baskets full; or twelve basketfuls were taken up.

6.45   Some manuscripts omit on the other side of the lake.
The other side: the west side.

6.46   to the people; or to the disciples.

6.48   pass them by; or join them.

6.53   Gennesaret: a fertile plain on the northwest shore of Lake Galilee.

6.56   The edge: the tassels which pious Jews wore on the edges of their cloaks as a sign of devotion to God (see Num 15.37-41; Matt 23.5).
it; or him.

7.1   Pharisees: see 2.16.
Teachers of the Law: see 1.22.

7.3   in the proper way; or carefully; or up to the wrist; or up to the elbow.

7.4   anything that comes from the market unless they wash it first;

or anything after they come from the market unless they wash themselves first.
wash; some manuscripts have sprinkle.
Some manuscripts omit and beds.

7.6-7   Isaiah...wrote: this quotation from Isa 29.13 follows the Septuagint, but is not identical with it.

7.9   uphold; some manuscripts have obey.

7.10   Moses commanded: see Exo 20.12; 21.17.

7.11   Corban: a Hebrew word.

7.15   Some manuscripts add verse 16: Listen, then, if you have ears! (see 4.23).

7.19   Fit to be eaten: no food is to be considered to make the person who eats it ritually unclean.

7.24   Tyre: see 3.8.
Some manuscripts add and Sidon (see Matt 15.21).

7.25   Evil spirit: see 1.23.

7.28   Sir; some manuscripts have That's true, sir (see Matt 15.27).

7.31   Tyre...Sidon: see 3.8.
Lake Galilee: see 1.16.
The Ten Towns: see 5.20.

7.34   Ephphatha: a transliteration of the Aramaic word spoken by Jesus.

8.8-9   the disciples took up seven baskets full; or seven basketfuls were taken up.

8.10   Dalmanutha: a place of uncertain location on the west shore of Lake Galilee.
Dalmanutha; some manuscripts have Magadan (see Matt 15.39); others have Magdala.

8.11   Pharisees: see 2.16.

8.13   The other side: the east side.

8.15   Pharisees: see 2.16.
Herod: Herod Antipas (see 6.14); some manuscripts have Herod's party (see 3.6).

8.22   Bethsaida: probably Bethsaida Julias, on the northeast shore of Lake Galilee.

8.24   looked up; or began to see.

8.26   Some manuscripts add Don't tell anyone in the village.

8.27   Caesarea Philippi: a city some 40 kilometers north of Lake
Galilee.

8.28   Elijah: see 6.15.
        Prophets: see 6.4.

8.29   Messiah: the title (the same as Christ) of the promised Savior
whose coming was foretold by the Hebrew prophets.

8.31   Son of Man: see 2.10.
        Elders: respected Jewish religious leaders, some of whom were
members of the Supreme Council.
        Chief priests: a group composed of the High Priest, former High
Priests still living, and the members of important families from
which the High Priests were chosen.
        Teachers of the Law: see 1.22.

8.33   Satan: see 1.13.

8.38   my teaching; some manuscripts have my followers.
        with; some manuscripts have and of.

9.1   Kingdom of God: see 1.15.

9.7   This is my own dear Son--listen to him!: these words reflect
such Old Testament passages as Psa 2.7; Gen 22.2; Deut 18.15.
        own dear Son; or only Son; or Son, the Beloved.

9.9   Son of Man: see 2.10.

9.11   Teachers of the Law: see 1.22.
        Elijah: see 6.15.

9.12   The Scriptures: the Hebrew Bible.

9.13   Elijah has already come: a reference to John the Baptist, who
was the fulfillment of God's promise to send the prophet Elijah to
prepare the way for the Messiah (see 6.15).

9.14   Teachers of the Law: see 1.22.

9.17   Evil spirit: see 1.23.

9.18   Drive...out: see 1.34.

9.29   prayer; some manuscripts add and fasting.

9.30   Galilee: see 1.19.

9.31   Son of Man: see 2.10.

9.33   Capernaum: see 1.21.

9.38   a man; some manuscripts add who doesn't belong to our group.
Driving out: see 1.34.
Demons: see 1.32.

9.42   Some manuscripts omit in me.

9.43   Some manuscripts add verse 44: There 'the worms that eat them
never die, and the fire that burns them is never put out' (see
verse 48).

9.45   Some manuscripts add verse 46: There 'the worms that eat them
never die, and the fire that burns them is never put out' (see
verse 48).

9.47   Kingdom of God: see 1.15.

9.48   The worms that: a free quotation from Isa 66.24.

9.49   A sacrifice is purified by salt: see Lev 2.13.

9.50   Have the salt...and live; or You have the salt...so live.

10.1   Judea: see 1.5.
Crossed: to the east side.

10.2   Pharisees: see 2.16.
Our Law: see 2.24.

10.4   Moses gave permission: see Deut 24.1.

10.6   The scripture says: see Gen 1.27.

10.7   Some manuscripts omit and unite with his wife.

10.7-8   And for this reason: see Gen 2.24.

10.14   Kingdom of God: see 1.15.

10.19   The commandments: see Exo 20.12-16; "do not cheat" is not in
the list of commandments.

10.24   how hard it is; some manuscripts add for those who trust in
riches.
Kingdom of God: see 1.15.

10.26   one another; some manuscripts have him.

10.33   Son of Man: see 2.10.
Chief priests: see 8.31.
Teachers of the Law: see 1.22.
The Gentiles: the Roman authorities.

10.45   Son of Man: see 2.10.

10.46   Jericho: a city west of the Jordan, some 24 kilometers northeast of Jerusalem.

10.47   Jesus of Nazareth: see 1.24.
Son of David: a title the Jews used of the promised Savior as
the descendant and successor of King David.

11.1   Bethphage: near the Mount of Olives.
Bethany: about 3 kilometers east of Jerusalem.
Mount of Olives: just to the east of Jerusalem, across Kidron
Valley.

11.2   The village: either Bethphage or Bethany (see verse 1).

11.3   The Master; or its owner.

11.9-10   See Psa 118.25-26.

11.15   Who were buying and selling: for the convenience of those who
came from distant places, animals fit for being offered in
sacrifice were sold in the Temple area.
Moneychangers: men who exchanged foreign currency into the
proper coin for paying the Temple tax and for buying animals to
be offered as sacrifice.

11.16   Anyone carry anything: many would use the Temple courtyards as
a short cut between the city and the Mount of Olives.

11.17   God said: see Isa 56.7.
Hideout for thieves: see Jer 7.11.

11.18   Chief priests: see 8.31.
Teachers of the Law: see 1.22.

11.19   Jesus and his disciples; some manuscripts have he.

11.22   Have faith in God; some manuscripts have If you have faith in
God, or Do you have faith in God?

11.25   Some manuscripts add verse 26: If you do not forgive others,
your Father in heaven will not forgive the wrongs you have done
(see Matt 6.15).

11.27   Chief priests: see 8.31.
Teachers of the Law: see 1.22.
Elders: see 8.31.

11.32   Prophet: see 6.4.

12.1   Parables: see 3.23.

12.6   own dear son; or only son.

12.10-11 This scripture: see Psa 118.22-23.

12.13   Pharisees: see 2.16.
         Herod's party: see 3.6.

12.14   Our Law: see 2.24.
         Roman Emperor: at that time Tiberius, who ruled A.D. 14-37.

12.15   A silver coin: a Roman coin called denarius.

12.18   Sadducees: a small Jewish group, composed largely of priests,
         who based their beliefs primarily on the first five books of the
         Hebrew Scriptures.

12.19   Moses wrote this law: see Deut 25.5-6.

12.23   Some manuscripts omit when all the dead rise to life.

12.24   Scriptures: see 9.12.

12.26   God said: see Exo 3.2-6.
         Book of Moses: the first five books of the Hebrew Scriptures.

12.28   Teacher of the Law: see 1.22.
         Sadducees: see 12.18.

12.29-30 The most important one: see Deut 6.4-5; "with all your mind"
         is not in the Old Testament passage.

12.29   The Lord our God is the only Lord; or The Lord is our God, the
         Lord alone; or The Lord our God is one Lord.

12.31   The second most important commandment: see Lev 19.18.

12.34   Kingdom of God: see 1.15.

12.35   Teachers of the Law: see 1.22.
         Messiah: see 8.29.

12.36   David to say: see Psa 110.1.
         Right side: the place of honor and authority.
         under; some manuscripts have as a footstool under.
         Under your feet: a figure of defeat and humiliation.

12.38   Teachers of the Law: see 1.22.

12.39   Synagogues: see 1.21.

12.41   sat; some manuscripts have stood.
         Temple treasury: the place where were located the boxes for
         the money.

13.3   Mount of Olives: see 11.1.

13.9   Synagogues: see 1.21.

13.14   The Awful Horror: the expression, as translated into Greek by
the Septuagint of Dan 11.31; 12.11, referring to the heathen altar
set up in the Temple by the Syrian king Antiochus Epiphanes in
167 B.C.; here a person is meant.
        Reader: the person who read the passage aloud to the assembled
congregation.
        Judea: see 1.5.

13.15   Roof: flat, reached by outside steps (see 2.4), a place where
people would go at the end of the day for rest and relaxation.

13.21   Messiah: see 8.29.

13.22   Prophets: see 6.4.

13.25   The powers in space: the stars and planets, which were believed
to be controlled by spiritual powers.

13.29   the time is near, ready to begin; or he (the Son of Man) is
near, ready to come.

13.33   be alert; some manuscripts add and pray.

14.1   Festival of Passover and Unleavened Bread: Passover was a
festival held on the 14th day of Nisan (around April 1), which
celebrated the deliverance of the ancient Hebrews from their
slavery in Egypt; Unleavened Bread, celebrating the same event,
was held Nisan 15-22; its name came from the practice of not
using leaven (yeast) in making bread during that week. The two
festivals were celebrated as one.
        Chief priests: see 8.31.
        Teachers of the Law: see 1.22.

14.3   Bethany: see 11.1.
        Dreaded skin disease: see 1.40.
        Alabaster: a soft stone of light, creamy color, from which
vases and jars were made.
        Nard: oil made from the root of the nard, a plant native to
India.

14.5   Silver coins: see 6.37.

14.8   Burial: the Jews used perfumed oils to prepare a body for
burial (see 16.1).

14.10   Chief priests: see 8.31.

14.12   Unleavened Bread: see 14.1.
        Passover: see 14.1.

14.13   The city: Jerusalem.

14.20   the dish; some manuscripts have the same dish.
The dish: the one that held the sauces into which the bread
was dipped.

14.21   Son of Man: see 2.10.
Scriptures: see 9.12.

14.24   covenant; some manuscripts have new covenant (see Luke 22.20).
Blood which seals God's covenant: God's covenant with the
people of Israel was sealed by the blood of the sacrificed animals
being sprinkled on the people (Exo 24.7-8).

14.25   Kingdom of God: see 1.15.

14.26   A hymn: Psalms 115-118 were customarily sung at the end of the
Passover meal.
Mount of Olives: see 11.1.

14.27   The scripture says: see Zech 13.7; there God commands his sword
to kill the shepherd.

14.32   Gethsemane: a garden on the western slope of the Mount of Olives.

14.41   Are you still sleeping and resting?; or Keep on sleeping and
resting.
Enough; or It is done.
Son of Man: see 2.10.

14.43   Chief priests: see 8.31.
Teachers of the Law: see 1.22.
Elders: see 8.31.

14.47   High Priest: see 2.26.

14.49   Scriptures: see 9.12.

14.53   High Priest: see 2.26.
Chief priests: see 8.31.
Elders: see 8.31.
Teachers of the Law: see 1.22.

14.55   Council: the supreme religious court of the Jews, composed of
about seventy leaders and presided over by the High Priest.

14.58   after; or in.

14.61   Messiah: see 8.29.

14.62   Son of Man: see 2.10.
The right side: see 12.36.

(34)

14.63   Tore his robes: a ritual act expressing outrage and horror.

14.66   High Priest: see 2.26.

14.67   Jesus of Nazareth: see 1.24.

14.68   Some manuscripts omit Just then a rooster crowed.

14.72   broke down; or thought about it; or ran out; or covered his
head.

15.1   Chief priests: see 8.31.
Elders: see 8.31.
Teachers of the Law: see 1.22.
Council: see 14.55.
Pilate: Pontius Pilate, the Roman governor of Judea, Samaria,
and Idumea, A.D. 26-36.

15.2   So you say; or Yes, it is as you say.

15.6   Passover: see 14.1.

15.7   The riot: apparently a well known event at that time, about
which nothing is now known.

15.8   gathered; some manuscripts have shouted.

15.10   Chief priests: see 8.31.

15.12   Some manuscripts omit the one you call.

15.16   Soldiers: Roman occupation troops.

15.21   Cross: here the horizontal beam which the condemned man was
forced to carry to the place of execution.
Cyrene: the capital of Libya, a country in North Africa.

15.27   bandits; or insurrectionists.
Some manuscripts add verse 28: In this way the scripture came
true which says, "He shared the fate of criminals" (see Luke 22.37).

15.31   Chief priests: see 8.31.
Teachers of the Law: see 1.22.

15.32   Messiah: see 8.29.

15.33   country; or world.

15.34   Eloi, Eloi, lema sabachthani: a transliteration of the Aramaic
form of the words of Psa 22.1.

15.35   Elijah: in Aramaic "Elijah" and "Eloi" sound somewhat alike;
and see 6.15.

(35)

15.38   Curtain: the large curtain separating the Holy Place from the
Most Holy Place.

15.39   had died; some manuscripts have had cried out and died.

15.40   Magdalene: from Magdala, a town on the west side of Lake Galilee.

15.42-43 Toward evening: before sunset, when the Sabbath would begin.
Arimathea: a town some 35 kilometers northwest of Jerusalem.
Council: see 14.55.
Kingdom of God: see 1.15.
Preparation: the day on which preparation was made for the
Sabbath, when no work could be done.

15.44   had been dead a long time; some manuscripts have had already
died.

15.47   Magdalene: see 15.40.
Joseph: the one mentioned in verse 40.

16.1   After the Sabbath was over: after sunset of that day.
Magdalene: see 15.40.
James: the one mentioned in 15.40.
Spices: aromatic oils used by Jews in preparing a body for
burial.

16.5   A young man...wearing a white robe: the customary description
of an angel.

16.6   Jesus of Nazareth: see 1.24.

16.7   As he told you: see 14.28.

16.9   Section Heading: AN OLD ENDING TO THE GOSPEL: Some manuscripts
and ancient translations omit this ending to the Gospel (verses
9-20).
Magdalene: see 15.40.
Driven out...demons: see 1.34.

16.10   Companions: the disciples.

16.17   Drive out demons: see 1.34.

16.19   The right side: see 12.36.

Section Heading: ANOTHER OLD ENDING: Some manuscripts and ancient translations have this shorter ending to the Gospel in addition
to the longer ending (verses 9-20).

LUKE

1.1   Theophilus: the person to whom the book is dedicated (also Acts 1.1); nothing definite is known about him, except that he was of high rank (verse 3) and knew the facts of the gospel (verse 4).

1.5   Herod: Herod the Great, king of all the land of Israel 37-4 B.C.
Judea: the term here refers to the whole land of Palestine.
Abijah: see 1 Chr 24.10.

1.17   Elijah: see Mal 4.5-6.

1.23   Period of service: one week (see 1 Chr 24.19).

1.25   Disgrace: it was considered a disgrace for a Jewish wife to be barren.

1.26   Nazareth: a town about 26 kilometers west of the southern edge of Lake Galilee.
Galilee: in the north, one of the provinces into which the country was divided.

1.28   Peace be with you: the customary greeting.
Some manuscripts add most blessed of all women (see verse 42).

1.31   Jesus: this name in Hebrew means "he saves" or "the Lord is savior."

1.35   the holy child; or the child will be holy and.

1.39   Judea: a province in the southern part of the country.

1.46-55 This song of praise is traditionally called the "Magnificat," the first word of the translation in Latin.

1.59   Circumcise: to cut off the foreskin of a Jewish baby boy as a sign of God's covenant with the people of Israel (see Gen 17.9-14).

1.68-79 This prophecy is traditionally called the "Benedictus," the first word of the translation in Latin.

1.76   Prophet: a person who proclaims God's message.

1.80   The desert: the desolate region on the west side of the Jordan, not far from where it empties into the Dead Sea.

2.1   Augustus: one of the titles of Gaius Octavius, who was Roman Emperor from 27 B.C. to A.D. 14.

2.2   When this...Quirinius; or This was the first census taken while Quirinius.
Syria: the land of Israel was then part of the Roman province of Syria.

2.4   Nazareth: see 1.26.
Bethlehem: about 8 kilometers south of Jerusalem.

2.7   Cloths: cloth strips which were wrapped around a newborn child.

2.11   David's town: Bethlehem (see verse 4).

2.14   peace...pleased; or peace on earth and God's good will for all people.

2.21   Circumcised: see 1.59.

2.22   The Law of Moses commanded: see Lev 12.2-4.

2.23   The law of the Lord: see Exo 13.2.

2.24   The law of the Lord: see Lev 12.8.

2.26   Messiah: the title (the same as Christ) of the promised Savior whose coming was foretold by the Hebrew prophets.

2.29-32 Simeon's prayer of praise is traditionally called the "Nunc Dimittis," the first two words of the translation in Latin.

2.32   Gentiles: people who are not Jews.

2.33   The child's father and mother; some manuscripts have Joseph and the child's mother.

2.36-37 was now eighty-four years old; or had been a widow eighty-four years.

2.37   Fasting: to go without food for a while as a religious duty.

2.41   Passover: a festival held on the 14th day of Nisan (around April 1), which celebrated the deliverance of the ancient Hebrews from their slavery in Egypt.

2.52   body; or age.

3.1   Tiberius: Roman Emperor A.D. 14-37; the fifteenth year of his rule would be around A.D. 28 or 29.
Pontius Pilate: Roman governor of the provinces of Judea, Samaria, and Idumea, A.D. 26-36.
Herod: Herod Antipas, ruler of the provinces of Galilee and Perea, 4 B.C.--A.D. 39.
Philip: ruler 4 B.C.--A.D. 34; Iturea and Trachonitis were regions in the northeastern part of the country.
Lysanias: nothing further is known about him; Abilene was a region west of Iturea.

3.2   Annas and Caiaphas: Annas had been the High Priest from about A.D. 6 to 15; his son-in-law Caiaphas occupied the office A.D. 18-36.

High Priest: the priest who occupied the highest office in the Jewish priestly system and who was president of the Supreme Council of the Jews.
Desert: see 1.80.

3.4-6   The prophet Isaiah: see Septuagint Isa 40.3-5; in verse 3 "for him" replaces "for our God" in Isa 40.3.

3.11   Shirt: a short-sleeved knee-length garment that was worn next to the body.

3.12   Tax collectors: men who collected taxes for the Roman government on goods or produce taken in or out of the town.

3.14   Soldiers: Roman occupation troops.

3.15   Messiah: see 2.26.

3.16   Untie his sandals: a menial task performed by a servant.

3.19   Herod: Herod Antipas (see 3.1).
His brother: Herod's half-brother Philip (see Mark 6.17) who lived in Rome (not to be confused with the Philip mentioned in 3.1).

3.22   You are my own dear Son. I am pleased with you: these words reflect such Old Testament passages as Psa 2.7; Gen 22.2; Isa 42.1.
Some manuscripts have You are my Son; today I have become your Father (see Psa 2.7).
my own dear Son; or my only Son; or my Son, the Beloved.

4.1   Desert: see 1.80.

4.2   Devil: the ruler of the forces of evil; the name means "the accuser."

4.4   The scripture says: see Deut 8.3.

4.8   The scripture says: see Deut 6.13.

4.10-11 The scripture says: see Psa 91.11-12.

4.12   The scripture says: see Deut 6.16.

4.13   for a while; or until the right time.

4.14   Galilee: see 1.26.

4.15   Taught: during the synagogue service anyone, ordained or not, could be asked to instruct the people in the explanation and application of the Hebrew Scriptures.
Synagogues: the public meeting houses where Jews gathered on the Sabbath for worship.

4.16   Nazareth: see 1.26.
        Sabbath: the seventh day of the Jewish week, the holy day on
which no work was allowed.
        Synagogue: see 4.15.
        Stood up to read: the presiding officer could ask any adult
male Jew to read the Scriptures in the worship service.
        Scriptures: the Hebrew Bible.

4.17-19 The prophet Isaiah: see Septuagint Isa 61.1-2; "to set free the
        oppressed" in verse 18 is from Isa 58.6.

4.25-26 Elijah: see 1 Kgs 17.1.

4.27   Elisha: see 2 Kgs 5.1-14.
        Dreaded skin disease: traditionally taken to be leprosy, but
probably the biblical term included other skin diseases as well
(see Lev 13.1-46; 14.1-32).

4.31   Capernaum: a town on the northwest shore of Lake Galilee.
        Taught: see 4.15.
        Sabbath: see 4.16.

4.33   Synagogue: see 4.15.
        Spirit of an evil demon: also called unclean spirit. Evil
spirits were regarded as being able to dominate people, and they
were called "unclean" because they caused certain bodily disorders
or actions which made people ritually defiled and thus prevented
them from taking part in public worship until their defilement
had been removed.

4.34   Jesus of Nazareth: frequently a person was identified by the
place he was from: for example, Elijah of Tishbe (1 Kgs 17.1);
Joseph of Arimathea (Mark 15.43); Saul of Tarsus (Acts 9.11).
        What do you want with us?: an idiomatic phrase (see Septuagint
Judges 11.12; 2 Sam 16.10; 1 Kgs 17.18) expressing hostility.
        Us: probably of all the evil spirits as a class.
        God's holy messenger; or God's Holy One. Probably used as a
title for the Messiah.

4.38   Synagogue: see 4.15.

4.40   After sunset: the Jewish day ended at sunset, and now that the
Sabbath (verse 31) was over, people were allowed to engage in
normal activities.

4.41   Demons: see 4.33.
        Messiah: see 2.26.

4.43   Kingdom of God: God's rule over mankind and the world. Sometimes
it is spoken of as a present reality, at other times as a future
event; in some instances it is equivalent to eternal life with God.

4.44   Synagogues: see 4.15.
        the country; or Judea; some manuscripts have Galilee (see
Mark 1.39).

5.1   Lake Gennesaret: Lake Galilee, a body of fresh water in the
province of Galilee, some 21 kilometers long and 13 kilometers
wide at its widest.

5.12   Dreaded skin disease: see 4.27.
        Make me clean: this disease was considered to make a person
ritually unclean.

5.13   Touched: all physical contact was to be avoided with a person
suffering from this disease.

5.14   Priest: either a local priest or one in the Temple in Jerusalem.
        The sacrifice as Moses ordered: see Lev 14.1-32.

5.17   Pharisees: a Jewish religious party whose members were strict
in obeying the Law of Moses and other regulations which had been
added to it through the centuries.
        Teachers of the Law: professionals who interpreted the Old
Testament, particularly the first five books.
        Galilee: see 1.26.
        Judea: see 1.39.
        for Jesus to heal the sick; some manuscripts have to heal them.

5.19   Roof: outside steps led up to the flat roof of Palestinian
homes.

5.20   Faith they had: of the men carrying the bed, and probably of
the sick man himself, in Jesus' power to heal.

5.24   Son of Man: a title of dignity, used only of Jesus in the New
Testament. In some passages it refers to the future coming of
Jesus in power.

5.27   Tax collector: see 3.12.
        Levi: called Matthew in Matt 9.9.

5.30   Pharisees and...teachers of the Law: see 5.17.
        Other outcasts: people who like the tax collectors were des-
pised by the religious leaders because of their refusal to obey
all the religious rules, especially those which prohibited eating
certain foods and associating with Gentiles.

5.32   respectable; or good.

5.33   Fast: to abstain temporarily from food as a religious duty.
        Pharisees: see 5.17.

5.34   guests at a wedding party; or a bridegroom's attendants.

(41)

5.36   Parable: a story using everyday matters to teach spiritual
        lessons.

6.1   Sabbath: see 4.16.
        Sabbath; some manuscripts have second-first Sabbath, which may
        mean the second Sabbath after the first, or the second Sabbath of
        the first month.

6.2   Our Law: the Hebrew Scriptures, especially the first five
        books; reaping was forbidden on the Sabbath (see Exo 34.21).

6.3-4   What David did: see 1 Sam 21.1-6.
        House of God: the Tent of the Lord's presence (see Exo 36.8-38).
        The bread offered to God: see Lev 24.5-9.

6.5   Son of Man: see 5.24.

6.6   Sabbath: see 4.16.
        Synagogue: see 4.15.

6.7   Teachers of the Law and...Pharisees: see 5.17.

6.9   Our Law: see 6.2.

6.10   said; some manuscripts have said angrily (see Mark 3.5).

6.13   Apostles: men who were commissioned to speak and act with the
        authority of the one who sent them.

6.15   Patriot: so called perhaps because he was, or had been, a
        member of a nationalist party which advocated the overthrow of
        the Roman authority by force if necessary.

6.17   Judea; or the whole country (see 1.5).
        Tyre and Sidon: Gentile cities on the Mediterranean coast, north
        of Galilee.

6.18   Evil spirits: see 4.33.

6.20   Kingdom of God: see 4.43.

6.22   Son of Man: see 5.24.

6.23   Prophets: God's messengers who proclaimed his message to the
        people of Israel.

6.29   Shirt: see 3.11.

6.35   and expect nothing back; some manuscripts have don't lose
        confidence in anyone.

6.39   Parable: see 5.36.

6.41   Brother: here a member of the same religious group.

6.48   well built; some manuscripts have built on rock (see Matt 7.25).

7.1   Capernaum: see 4.31.

7.2   Roman officer: probably the army officer in charge of the local Roman occupation troops.

7.3   Elders: respected Jewish religious leaders, some of whom were members of the Supreme Council.

7.5   Synagogue: see 4.15.

7.11   Soon afterward; some manuscripts have The next day.
Nain: a town some 10 kilometers southeast of Nazareth.

7.16   Prophet: see 1.76.
all the country; or Judea (see 1.5).

7.21   Evil spirits: see 4.33.
Dreaded skin diseases: see 4.27.
Made clean: see 5.12.

7.26   Prophet: see 1.76.

7.27   The scripture says: see Mal 3.1; "ahead of you" may be from Exo 23.20.

7.28   greater than any man; some manuscripts have the greatest prophet.
Kingdom of God: see 4.43.

7.29   Tax collectors: see 3.12.

7.30   Pharisees and the teachers of the Law: see 5.17.

7.33   Fasted: see 5.33.
Demon: see 4.33.

7.34   Son of Man: see 5.24.
Other outcasts: see 5.30.

7.36   Pharisee: see 5.17.

7.37   Alabaster: a soft stone of light, creamy color, from which vases and jars were made.

7.38   Behind Jesus, by his feet: at that time people at a meal reclined on cushions, with their legs stretched out behind them.

7.39   Prophet: see 1.76.

7.46   Olive oil for my head: it was the custom at that time for a host to provide olive oil for his guest to rub on his hair and face, after coming in from the hot, dusty road.

8.1   Kingdom of God: see 4.43.

8.2   Evil spirits: see 4.33.
        Magdalene: from Magdala, a town on the west shore of Lake Galilee.

8.3   Herod: Herod Antipas, ruler of Galilee (see 3.1).
        Jesus and his disciples; some manuscripts have Jesus.

8.4   Parable: see 5.36.

8.9   Kingdom of God: see 4.43.

8.12   Devil: see 4.2.

8.16   Lamp: an oil-burning wick lamp, the wick lying in a shallow clay bowl filled with olive oil.

8.22   The other side: the east side.
        The lake: Lake Galilee (see 5.1).

8.26   Gerasa; some manuscripts have Gadara (see Matt 8.28); others have Gergesa.
        Gerasa: a Gentile town, apparently some 60 kilometers southeast of Lake Galilee.

8.27   Demons: see 4.33.
        What do you want with me?: see 4.34.

8.31   Abyss: it was thought that the demons were to be imprisoned in the depths of the earth until their final punishment.

8.34   The town: Gerasa (see verse 26).

8.40   The other side: the west side.

8.41   Synagogue: see 4.15.

8.43   Severe bleeding: due to menstrual disorder.
        Some manuscripts omit she had spent all she had on doctors.

8.44   The edge: the tassels which pious Jews wore on the edges of their cloaks as a sign of their devotion to God (see Num 15.37-41; Matt 23.5).

8.45   Peter; some manuscripts add and his companions.

8.48   My daughter: an expression of endearment.

9.1   Drive out...demons: see 4.33.

9.2   Kingdom of God: see 4.43.

9.4   Shirt: see 3.11.

9.5   Shake the dust off your feet: a sign of complete rejection.

9.7   Herod: Herod Antipas (see 3.1).

9.8   Elijah: a Hebrew prophet the Jews expected to return and prepare the way for the Messiah (see Mal 4.5-6).
Prophets: see 1.76.

9.10   Apostles: see 6.13.
Came back: from the trip on which Jesus had sent them (see 9.1-6).
Bethsaida: a town on the northeast shore of Lake Galilee.

9.11   Kingdom of God: see 4.43.

9.17   the disciples took up twelve baskets; or twelve basketfuls were taken up.

9.19   Elijah: see 9.8.
Prophets: see 1.76.

9.20   Messiah: see 2.26.

9.22   Son of Man: see 5.24.
Elders: see 7.3.
Chief priests: a group composed of the High Priest, former High Priests still living, and the members of important families from which the High Priests were chosen.
Teachers of the Law: see 5.17.

9.26   teaching; some manuscripts have followers.

9.27   Kingdom of God: see 4.43.

9.35   This is my Son, whom I have chosen--listen to him!: these words reflect such Old Testament passages as Psa 2.7; Gen 22.2; Deut 18.15.
my Son, whom I have chosen; some manuscripts have my own dear Son (see Mark 9.7).

9.39   Spirit: see 4.33.

9.49   Driving out demons: see 4.33.

9.52   Samaria: the province between Judea and Galilee. There was much hostility between Jews and Samaritans because of differences in race, customs, politics, and religion.

9.54   Some manuscripts add as Elijah did.

9.55   Some manuscripts add and said, "You don't know what kind of a Spirit you belong to; for the Son of Man did not come to destroy men's lives, but to save them."

9.58   Son of Man: see 5.24.

9.59   Bury my father: an expression that probably means "take care of my father until he dies."

9.60   Kingdom of God: see 4.43.

10.1   seventy-two; some manuscripts have seventy.

10.5   Peace be with this house: the customary greeting.

10.9   Kingdom of God: see 4.43.
has come near you; or has come to you.

10.11   The dust...we wipe off: see 9.5.
has come near you; or has come to you.

10.12   Sodom: a city near the Dead Sea which God destroyed by fire because of the great wickedness of its people (see Gen 19.24-28).

10.13   Tyre and Sidon: see 6.17.

10.15   Did you...heaven? You will...hell: see Isa 14.13-15.

10.17   seventy-two; some manuscripts have seventy (see verse 1).
Demons: see 4.33.

10.18   Satan: another name for the Devil; it means "the opponent."

10.19   The Enemy: the Devil.

10.21   by the Holy Spirit; some manuscripts have by the Spirit; others have in his spirit.

10.22   Some manuscripts begin the verse Then Jesus turned to the disciples and said.

10.24   Prophets: see 6.23.

10.25   Teachers of the Law: see 5.17.

10.26   Scriptures: see 4.16.

10.27   Answered: see Deut 6.5; Lev 19.18; "with all your mind" is not in the passages cited.

10.30   Jericho: a city west of the Jordan, some 24 kilometers northeast of Jerusalem.

10.32   Levite: a member of the priestly tribe of Levi, who had the duty of helping in the services in the Temple (Num 3.1-13).

10.33   Samaritan: see 9.52.

10.34   Oil and wine: used as remedies, the olive oil to soothe the pain and the wine to disinfect the wound.

10.42   just one is needed; some manuscripts have only a few things are needed, or just one.

11.2   Kingdom: see 4.43.

11.3   the food we need; or food for the next day.

11.11   Some manuscripts add a stone when he asks for bread? or (see Matt 7.9).

11.14   Driving out a demon: see 4.33.

11.15   Beelzebul: the name given the Devil as the ruler of the evil spirits; it is probably related to the name of the Philistine god Baalzebub (see 2 Kgs 1.2-3).

11.18   Satan: see 10.18.

11.20   Kingdom of God: see 4.43.

11.24   Evil spirit: see 4.33.
Dry country: the desert was thought to be the place where evil spirits liked to live.

11.29-30 Jonah: see Jonah 3.

11.31   The Queen of Sheba: see 1 Kgs 10.1-10.

11.33   Lamp: see 8.16.
Some manuscripts omit or puts it under a bowl.

11.37   Pharisee: see 5.17.

11.38   washed; or bathed.

11.43   Synagogues: see 4.15.

11.45   Teacher of the Law: see 5.17.

11.47   Prophets: see 6.23.

11.51   Zechariah: see 2 Chr 24.20-22. This was the last murder reported in the Hebrew Scriptures (2 Chronicles is the last in the arrangement of books of the Hebrew Bible) as Abel's was the first (Gen 4.8).

12.8   Son of Man: see 5.24.

12.11   Synagogues: see 4.15.

12.25   live a bit longer; or grow a bit taller.

12.27   grow: they don't work or make clothes for themselves; some manuscripts have neither weave cloth nor make clothes for themselves.
     King Solomon: in his time he was the richest of all kings (1 Kgs 10.23).

12.31   Kingdom: see 4.43.

12.33   Moth: much of the wealth of that time consisted of expensive garments and rugs.

12.35   Lamps: see 8.16.

12.40   Son of Man: see 5.24.

12.41   Parable: see 5.36.

12.46   cut him in pieces; or throw him out.

13.1   Pilate: see 3.1.

13.4   Siloam: a suburb of Jerusalem.

13.6   Parable: see 5.36.

13.10   Sabbath: see 4.16.
     Teaching in a synagogue: see 4.15.

13.11   Evil spirit: see 4.33.

13.16   Satan: see 10.18.

13.18   Kingdom of God: see 4.43.

13.28   Kingdom of God: see 4.43.

13.31   Pharisees: see 5.17.
     Herod: Herod Antipas, ruler of Galilee (see 3.1).

13.32   Driving out demons: see 4.33.

13.33   Prophet: see 1.76.

14.1   Sabbath: see 4.16.
     Pharisees: see 5.17.

14.3   Teachers of the Law: see 5.17.
        Our Law: see 6.2.

14.5   son; some manuscripts have donkey (see 13.15).

14.15   Kingdom of God: see 4.43.

15.1   Tax collectors: see 3.12.
        Other outcasts: see 5.30.

15.2   Pharisees and the teachers of the Law: see 5.17.

15.3   Parable: see 5.36.

15.7   respectable; or good.

15.8   Lamp: see 8.16.

15.15   Pigs: animals which Jews were not allowed to eat because they
        were classified as impure by the Law (Deut 14.8).

15.16   anything to eat; or any.

15.21   Some manuscripts add treat me as one of your hired workers
        (see verse 19).

16.14   Pharisees: see 5.17.

16.16   The Law of Moses and the...prophets: respectively, the first
        five books of the Hebrew Scriptures and the second division of the
        Hebrew Scriptures. The phrase was often used to refer to the whole
        Hebrew Bible.
        Kingdom of God: see 4.43.

16.23   Hades: the world of the dead.

16.25   My son: an expression of endearment.

16.29   Moses and the prophets: see 16.16.

17.3   Brother: see 6.41.

17.5   Apostles: see 6.13.

17.12   Dreaded skin disease: see 4.27.

17.14   Priests: either local priests or those in the Temple in Jerusalem.
        Made clean: see 5.12.

17.16   Samaritan: see 9.52.

17.20   Pharisees: see 5.17.

Kingdom of God: see 4.43.

17.21   within you; or among you; or will suddenly appear among you.

17.22   Son of Man: see 5.24.

17.24   Some manuscripts omit in his day.

17.27   The flood: see Gen 7.6-23.

17.28-29 Lot: see Gen 19.15-25.

17.31   Roof: flat, reached by outside steps (see 5.19), a place where people would go at the end of the day for rest and relaxation.

17.32   Lot's wife: see Gen 19.26.

17.35   Some manuscripts add verse 36: Two men will be working in a field: one will be taken away, the other left behind (see Matt 24.40).

18.1   Parable: see 5.36.

18.8   Son of Man: see 5.24.

18.9   Parable: see 5.36.

18.10   Pharisee: see 5.17.
         Tax collector: see 3.12.

18.11   stood apart by himself and prayed; some manuscripts have stood up and prayed to himself.

18.12   Fast: see 5.33.
         Two days a week: the second and the fifth days.

18.16   Kingdom of God: see 4.43.

18.20   The commandments: see Exo 20.12-16.

18.24   saw that he was sad; some manuscripts have looked at him.
         Kingdom of God: see 4.43.

18.31   Prophets: see 6.23.
         Son of Man: see 5.24.

18.32   The Gentiles: the Roman authorities.

18.35   Jericho: see 10.30.

18.37   Jesus of Nazareth: see 4.34.

18.38   Son of David: a title the Jews used of the promised Savior as the descendant and successor of King David.

19.1   Jericho: see 10.30.

19.2   Tax collector: see 3.12.

19.10   Son of Man: see 5.24.

19.11   Parable: see 5.36.
        Kingdom of God: see 4.43.

19.25   Some manuscripts omit verse 25.

19.29   Bethphage: near the Mount of Olives.
        Bethany: about 3 kilometers east of Jerusalem.
        Mount of Olives: just to the east of Jerusalem, across Kidron
Valley.

19.30   The village: either Bethphage or Bethany (see verse 29).

19.31   the Master; or its owner.

19.37   Mount of Olives: see 19.29.

19.39   Pharisees: see 5.17.

19.45   Merchants: for the convenience of worshipers who came from
        distant places, animals fit for being offered in sacrifice were
        sold in the Temple area.

19.46   God said: see Isa 56.7.
        Hideout for thieves: see Jer 7.11.

19.47   Chief priests: see 9.22.
        Teachers of the Law: see 5.17.

20.1   Chief priests: see 9.22.
        Teachers of the Law: see 5.17.
        Elders: see 7.3.

20.6   Prophet: see 1.76.

20.9   Parable: see 5.36.

20.13   own dear son; or only son.

20.17   This scripture: see Psa 118.22.

20.19   Teachers of the Law: see 5.17.
        Chief priests: see 9.22.
        Parable: see 5.36.

20.22   Our Law: see 6.2.
        Roman Emperor: at that time Tiberius, who ruled A.D. 14-37.

(51)

20.23   Silver coin: a Roman coin called denarius.

20.27   Sadducees: a small Jewish group, composed largely of priests, who based their beliefs primarily on the first five books of the Hebrew Scriptures.

20.28   Moses wrote this law: see Deut 25.5-6.

20.37   The passage: see Exo 3.2-6.

20.39   Teachers of the Law: see 5.17.

20.41   Messiah: see 2.26.

20.42-43   David...says: see Psa 110.1.

20.42   Right side: the place of honor and authority.
A footstool under your feet: a figure of defeat and humiliation.

20.46   Teachers of the Law: see 5.17.
Synagogues: see 4.15.

21.1   Temple treasury: the boxes for the money (see Mark 12.41).

21.12   Synagogues: see 4.15.

21.22   Days of Punishment: the time when God will punish the people for their sins.

21.26   Powers in space: the stars and planets, which were believed to be controlled by spiritual powers.

21.31   Kingdom of God: see 4.43.

21.36   Son of Man: see 5.24.

21.37   Mount of Olives: see 19.29.

21.38   A few manuscripts add here the passage John 8.1-11.

22.1   Unleavened Bread: a festival celebrating the deliverance of the ancient Hebrews from their slavery in Egypt; it was held Nisan 15-22 (around the first part of April). Its name came from the practice of not using leaven (yeast) in making bread during that week.
Passover: a festival celebrating the same event; it was held on Nisan 14 (around April 1). The two festivals were celebrated as one.

22.2   Chief priests: see 9.22.
Teachers of the Law: see 5.17.

22.3   Satan: see 10.18.

(52)

22.4   Temple guard: Levites whose duty it was to guard and maintain order in the Temple.

22.7   Unleavened Bread...Passover: see 22.1.

22.10   The city: Jerusalem.

22.14   The hour: when the meal was eaten, after sundown.

22.16   Some manuscripts add again.
        Kingdom of God: see 4.43.

22.20   Covenant sealed with my blood: God's covenant with the people of Israel was sealed by blood of the sacrificed animals being sprinkled on the people (Exo 24.7-8).
        Some manuscripts omit the words of Jesus after This is my body in verse 19, and all of verse 20.

22.22   Son of Man: see 5.24.

22.31   Satan: see 10.18.

22.32   Brothers: see 6.41.

22.35   I sent you out: see Luke 10.4.

22.37   The scripture: see Isa 53.12.

22.38   That is enough; or Enough of this.

22.39   Mount of Olives: see 19.29.

22.44   Some manuscripts omit verses 43-44.

22.52   Chief priests: see 9.22.
        Temple guard: see 22.4.
        Elders: see 7.3.

22.54   High Priest: Caiaphas (see 3.2).

22.59   Galilean: from his accent (see Matt 26.73).

22.66   Elders: see 7.3.
        Chief priests: see 9.22.
        Teachers of the Law: see 5.17.
        Council: the supreme religious court of the Jews, composed of about seventy leaders and presided over by the High Priest.

22.67   Messiah: see 2.26.

22.69   Son of Man: see 5.24.
        Right side: see 20.42.

22.70   You say that I am; or Yes I am, as you say.

23.1   Pilate: see 3.1.

23.2   Messiah: see 2.26.

23.3   So you say; or Yes, it is as you say.

23.4   Chief priests: see 9.22.

23.5   Judea: see 1.39.
        Galilee: see 1.26.

23.7   Herod: Herod Antipas (see 3.1).

23.10   Chief priests: see 9.22.
        Teachers of the Law: see 5.17.

23.16   Some manuscripts add verse 17: At every Passover Festival
        Pilate had to set free one prisoner for them (see Mark 15.6).

23.26   Soldiers: Roman soldiers.
        Cyrene: the capital of Libya, a country in North Africa.
        Cross: here the horizontal beam which the condemned man was
        forced to carry to the place of execution.

23.34   Some manuscripts omit Jesus said, "Forgive them, Father! They
        don't know what they are doing."

23.35   Messiah: see 2.26.

23.38   Some manuscripts add in Greek, Latin, and Hebrew (see John 19.20).

23.44   country; or world.

23.45   Curtain: the large curtain separating the Holy Place from the
        Most Holy Place.

23.46   In your hands: see Psa 31.5.

23.47   he was a good man; or this man was innocent.

23.49   Galilee: see 1.26.

23.50-51 Arimathea: some 35 kilometers northwest of Jerusalem.
        Kingdom of God: see 4.43.
        Council: see 22.66.

23.52   Pilate: see 3.1.

23.54   Sabbath: see 4.16.
        About to begin: the day began at sundown.

24.4   Men in bright shining clothes: the customary description of angels (see 24.23).

24.6   Some manuscripts omit He is not here; he has been raised.

24.6-7 What he said: see Luke 18.32-33.
        Son of Man: see 5.24.

24.10 Magdalene: see 8.2.
       mother; or wife.
       Apostles: see 6.13.

24.12 Some manuscripts omit verse 12.

24.13 seven miles; some manuscripts have nineteen miles.

24.19 Jesus of Nazareth: see 4.34.
       Prophet: see 1.76.

24.20 Chief priests: see 9.22.

24.26 Messiah: see 2.26.

24.27 Scriptures: see 4.16.
       Books of Moses and...the prophets: see 16.16.

24.36 Peace be with you: the customary greeting.
       Some manuscripts omit and he said to them, "Peace be with you."

24.40 Some manuscripts omit verse 40.

24.42 Some manuscripts add and a piece of a honeycomb.

24.44 Law of Moses...the prophets, and the Psalms: the whole of the Hebrew Scriptures, which consist of three divisions: Moses, the Prophets, and the Writings (of which the Psalms are the first book).

24.46 Messiah: see 2.26.

24.49 What my Father has promised: the Holy Spirit (see Acts 1.4-5).
       The city: Jerusalem.

24.50 Bethany: see 19.29.

24.51 Some manuscripts omit and was taken up into heaven.

24.52 Some manuscripts omit worshiped him and.

JOHN

1.1   The Word: the expression of the creative and saving power and wisdom of God (see Psa 33.6,9; 107.19-20; Prov 8.22-31), which became a human being in Jesus Christ (verse 14).

1.4   The Word was the source of life; or What was made had life in union with the Word.

1.5   Darkness: the powers of evil and destruction.
put it out; or understood it.

1.11   His own country...his own people: the land and the people of Israel.

1.14   Glory: the manifestation of God's presence and power (see Exo 24.16).

1.19   Levites: members of the priestly tribe of Levi, who had the duty of helping in the Temple services (see Num 3.1-13).

1.20   Messiah: the title (the same as Christ) of the promised Savior whose coming was foretold by the Hebrew prophets.

1.21   Elijah: a Hebrew prophet the Jews expected to return and prepare the way for the Messiah (see Mal 4.5-6).
The Prophet: the one who was expected to appear and announce the coming of the Messiah.

1.23   The prophet Isaiah: see Septuagint Isa 40.3.

1.24   Pharisees: a Jewish religious party whose members were strict in obeying the Law of Moses and other regulations which had been added to it through the centuries.

1.25   The messengers, who had been sent by the Pharisees, then; or Those who had been sent were Pharisees; they.

1.27   Untie his sandals: a menial task performed by a slave.

1.28   Bethany: not to be confused with the one near Jerusalem (11.18).

1.34   the Son of God; some manuscripts have the one chosen by God.

1.40   Messiah: see 1.20.

1.42   Cephas...Peter: the Aramaic and the Greek forms of the name; Jesus probably spoke in Aramaic and the Gospel was written in Greek.

1.44   Bethsaida: on the northeast shore of Lake Galilee.

1.45   The book of the Law...the prophets: respectively, the first
        five books of the Hebrew Scriptures and the second division of
        the Hebrew Scriptures. The whole phrase was often used to refer to
        the whole Hebrew Bible.
            Nazareth: a town about 26 kilometers west of the southern edge
        of Lake Galilee.

1.51   Angels going up and coming down: see Gen 28.12.
            Son of Man: a title of dignity, used only of Jesus in the New
        Testament.

2.1   Cana: a town some 6 kilometers north of Nazareth.
            Galilee: in the north, one of the provinces into which the
        country was divided.

2.4   My time: in this Gospel the hour when the true nature of Jesus
        will be revealed.

2.11   Glory: see 1.14.
            Capernaum: a town on the northwest shore of Lake Galilee.

2.13   Passover: a festival held on the 14th day of Nisan (around
        April 1), which celebrated the deliverance of the ancient Hebrews
        from their slavery in Egypt.

2.14   Men selling cattle, sheep, and pigeons: for the convenience of
        those who came from distant places, animals fit for being offered
        in sacrifice were sold in the Temple area.
            Moneychangers: men who exchanged foreign currency into the
        proper coin for paying the Temple tax and for buying animals to
        be offered as sacrifice.

2.17   The scripture: see Psa 69.9.

2.20   Forty-six years: the Temple was rebuilt by Herod the Great,
        beginning in 19 B.C., which would fix the date here at around
        A.D. 28.

2.23   Passover: see 2.13.

3.1   Pharisees: see 1.24.

3.2   Rabbi: Aramaic for "teacher" (see 1.38).

3.3   Kingdom of God: God's rule over mankind and the world.
            again; or from above.

3.7   again; or from above.

3.8   Wind...Spirit: a play on words; the same Greek word means both
        "wind" and "Spirit."

(57)

3.13 Son of Man: see 1.51.
Some manuscripts add and who is in heaven.

3.14 Moses: see Num 21.4-9.
Be lifted up: referring both to his crucifixion and his exaltation (see 12.32-33).

3.22 Judea: the province in the south of the country.

3.23 Aenon...Salim: two places whose exact locations are uncertain.

3.24 Prison: see Mark 6.17-18.

3.25 a Jew; some manuscripts have some Jews.

3.28 Messiah: see 1.20.

4.1 Pharisees: see 2.13.

4.3 Jesus; some manuscripts have the Lord.
Judea: see 3.22.
Galilee: see 2.1.

4.4 Samaria: the province between Judea and Galilee. There was much hostility between Jews and Samaritans because of differences in race, customs, politics, and religion.

4.5 Sychar: perhaps Shechem (see Gen 33.18-19), in the valley between Mt. Gerizim and Mt. Ebal; or perhaps another village, known as Askar, about one kilometer north of Jacob's well.
The field: see Gen 48.22; Josh 24.32.

4.9 Jews will not use the same cups and bowls that Samaritans use; or Jews will have nothing to do with Samaritans.

4.19 Prophet: a person who proclaims God's message.

4.20 This mountain: Mt. Gerizim (see verse 5).

4.25 Messiah: see 1.20.

4.43 Galilee: see 2.1.

4.44 Prophet: see 4.19.

4.45 Passover: see 2.13.

4.46 Cana: see 2.1.
Government official: in the service of Herod Antipas, ruler of the provinces of Galilee and Perea.
Capernaum: see 2.11.

4.54 Second miracle: see 2.11.

5.1   a religious festival; some manuscripts have the religious festival (which would probably be Passover; see 6.4).

5.2   Near the Sheep Gate...a pool; or Near the Sheep Pool...a place.
Sheep Gate: on the north side of the city.
Bethzatha; some manuscripts have Bethesda.

5.3   Some manuscripts add verses 3b-4: They were waiting for the water to move, 4because every now and then an angel of the Lord went down into the pool and stirred up the water. The first sick person to go into the pool after the water was stirred up was healed from whatever disease he had.

5.9   Sabbath: the seventh day of the Jewish week, the holy day on which no work was allowed.

5.10   Our Law: the Hebrew Scriptures, especially the first five books.

5.27   Son of Man: see 1.51.

5.39   You study; or Study.

5.44   the only one who is God; some manuscripts have the Only One.

5.46   Moses...wrote: a reference to the first five books of the Hebrew Scriptures.

6.1   Across: to the east side.
Lake Galilee: a body of fresh water in the province of Galilee, some 21 kilometers long and 13 kilometers wide at its widest.

6.4   Passover: see 2.13.

6.7   Silver coins: a silver coin was the daily wage of a rural worker (see Matt 20.2).

6.14   The Prophet: see 1.21.

6.17   Capernaum: see 2.11.

6.21   Then they willingly took him; or They were willing to take him.

6.22   The other side: the east side.

6.23   Tiberias: a town on the west side of Lake Galilee.
Some manuscripts omit after the Lord had given thanks.

6.24   Capernaum: see 2.11.

6.25   The other side: the west side.

6.27   Son of Man: see 1.51.

6.31   Ate manna: see Exo 16.4-15.
        The scripture says: see Septuagint Psa 78.24.

6.32   What Moses gave you was not; or It was not Moses who gave you.

6.45   The prophets wrote: see Septuagint Isa 54.13.

6.47   Some manuscripts add in me.

6.59   Synagogue: the public meeting house where Jews gathered on the
        Sabbath for worship.
        Capernaum: see 2.11.

6.62   Son of Man: see 1.51.

6.69   Holy One: probably a title for the Messiah.

7.1   Galilee: see 2.1.
        Judea: see 3.22.

7.2   Festival of Shelters: an eight-day festival, beginning on the
        15th day of Tishri (around October 6), which celebrated the time
        when the ancient Hebrews lived in simple shelters during their
        travels through the wilderness (see Lev 23.33-43).

7.8   I am not going; some manuscripts have I am not yet going.

7.20   Demon: an evil spiritual being who was regarded as being able
        to dominate people. In this Gospel, "You have a demon in you"
        means "You are crazy."

7.22   Circumcise: to cut off the foreskin of a Jewish baby boy as a
        sign of God's covenant with the people of Israel (see Gen 17.9-14).

7.23   I made a man completely well: the cure reported in 5.1-15.

7.26   Messiah: see 1.20.

7.30   His hour: see 2.4.

7.32   Pharisees: see 1.24.
        Chief priests: a group composed of the High Priest, former High
        Priests still living, and the members of important families from
        which the High Priests were chosen.
        Guards: Levites whose duty it was to guard and maintain order
        in the Temple.

7.37   Last...day of the festival: see 7.2.

7.38   Jesus' words in verses 37-38 may be translated: Whoever is
        thirsty should come to me, and whoever believes in me should drink.
        38As the scripture says, 'Streams of life-giving water will pour
        out from his heart.'

Scripture: there is no Old Testament passage that conforms to this quotation.

7.40   The Prophet: see 1.21.

7.41   Messiah: see 1.20.
        Bethlehem: in Judea, about 8 kilometers south of Jerusalem.

7.42   The scripture: see Micah 5.2.

7.45   Chief priests: see 7.32.
        Pharisees: see 1.24.

7.51   Our Law: see 5.10.

7.52   no prophet ever comes; one manuscript has the Prophet will not come.

8.1   Mount of Olives: just to the east of Jerusalem, across Kidron Valley.

8.3   Teachers of the Law: professionals who interpreted the Old Testament, particularly the first five books.
        Pharisees: see 1.24.

8.5   Moses commanded: see Deut 22.22.

8.11   Many manuscripts and early translations do not have this passage (8.1-11); others have it after John 21.24; others have it after Luke 21.38; one manuscript has it after John 7.36.

8.12   Pharisees: see 1.24.

8.17   Your Law: see Deut 19.15.

8.24   I Am Who I Am: an allusion to the name by which God made himself known to the people of Israel (see Exo 3.14).

8.25   What I have told you from the very beginning; or Why should I speak to you at all?

8.28   Lift up: see 3.14.
        Son of Man: see 1.51.

8.34   Some manuscripts omit of sin.

8.39   If you really were...you would do; some manuscripts have If you are...do.

8.48   Samaritan: see 4.4.
        Demon: see 7.20.

(61)

8.57   you have seen Abraham?; some manuscripts have has Abraham seen you?

8.58   I Am: see 8.24.

9.4   we; some manuscripts have I.

9.8   Siloam: a suburb of Jerusalem.

9.13   Pharisees: see 1.24.

9.14   Sabbath: see 5.9.

9.16   Sabbath law: work such as making mud (verse 14) was forbidden.

9.17   Prophet: see 4.19.

9.22   Messiah: see 1.20.
        Synagogue: see 6.59; a person expelled from the synagogue was no longer considered to belong to the people of God.

9.35   Son of Man: see 1.51.

9.40   Pharisees: see 1.24.

10.6   Parable: a story using everyday matters to teach a spiritual lesson.

10.16   they will become; some manuscripts have there will be.

10.20   Demon: see 7.20.

10.22   Festival of the Dedication: an eight-day festival, beginning on the 25th day of Kislev (around December 10), which celebrated the restoration and rededication of the Temple by the Jewish patriot Judas Maccabeus in 165 B.C. The Jewish name of the festival is Hanukkah.

10.23   Solomon's Porch: a colonnade on the east side of the Temple.

10.24   Messiah: see 1.20.

10.29   What my Father gave me is greater; some manuscripts have My Father, who gave them to me, is greater.

10.34   Your own Law: see 5.10.
        God said: see Psa 82.6.

10.40   The place: see 1.28.

11.1   Bethany: a town about 3 kilometers east of Jerusalem.

11.2   This Mary: see 12.1-8.

11.7   Judea: see 3.22.

11.27   Messiah: see 1.20.

11.40   God's glory: see 1.14.

11.46   Pharisees: see 1.24.

11.47   Chief priests: see 7.32.
        Council: the supreme religious court of the Jews, composed of
        about seventy leaders and presided over by the High Priest.

11.49   Caiaphas: the High Priest A.D. 18-36.
        High Priest: the priest who occupied the highest office in the
        Jewish priestly system and who was president of the Supreme Council
        of the Jews.

11.54   Judea: see 3.22.
        Ephraim: about 24 kilometers northeast of Jerusalem.

11.55   Passover: see 2.13.

12.1   Passover: see 2.13.
        Bethany: see 11.1.

12.5   Silver coins: see 6.7.

12.7   Let her keep what she has; or She has kept the perfume.

12.10   Chief priests: see 7.32.

12.12   Passover: see 2.13.

12.14-15 The scripture: see Isa 40.9; Zech 9.9.

12.19   Pharisees: see 1.24.

12.21   Bethsaida: see 1.44.

12.23   Son of Man: see 1.51.

12.31   The ruler of this world: the Devil, supreme lord of evil.

12.32   Lifted up: see 3.14.

12.34   Our Law: see 5.10.
        Messiah: see 1.20.
        Son of Man: see 1.51.

12.38   Isaiah had said: see Isa 53.1.

(63)

12.39-40 <u>Isaiah also said</u>: see Septuagint Isa 6.10; in the Hebrew Text the prophet is commanded to perform the actions: "Blind their eyes and close their minds"; in the Septuagint it is the people themselves who act: "They blinded their eyes and closed their minds"; here it is God who acts.

12.41 <u>because</u>; <u>some manuscripts have</u> when.

12.42 <u>Pharisees</u>: see 1.24.
<u>Synagogue</u>: see 9.22.

13.1 <u>Passover</u>: see 2.13.

13.2 The Devil...Simon Iscariot; <u>or</u> The Devil had already decided that Judas, the son of Simon Iscariot, would betray Jesus.

13.10 <u>Some manuscripts omit</u> except for his feet.

13.18 <u>The scripture</u>: see Psa 41.9.

13.19 <u>I Am Who I Am</u>: see 8.24.

13.31 <u>Son of Man</u>: see 1.51.

13.32 <u>Some manuscripts omit</u> if God's glory is revealed through him, then.

13.33 <u>My children</u>: an expression of endearment.
<u>What I told</u>: see 8.21.

13.36 <u>Later you will follow me</u>: a reference to Peter's death.

14.1 <u>Believe</u>; <u>or</u> You believe.

14.2 There are...were not so; <u>or</u> There are many rooms in my Father's house; if it were not so, would I tell you that I am going to prepare a place for you?

14.7 Now that you have known me...you will know; <u>some manuscripts have</u> If you had known me...you would know.

14.14 <u>Some manuscripts omit</u> me.

14.17 <u>is</u>; <u>some manuscripts have</u> will be.

14.30 <u>The ruler of this world</u>: see 12.31.

15.25 <u>Their Law</u>: see Psa 69.4.

16.2 <u>Synagogues</u>: see 9.22.

16.11 <u>The ruler of this world</u>: see 12.31.

16.23   the Father will give you whatever you ask of him in my name; some manuscripts have if you ask the Father for anything, he will give it to you in my name.

17.11   Keep them safe by the power of your name, the name you gave me; some manuscripts have By the power of your name keep safe those you have given me.

17.12   I kept them safe by the power of your name, the name you gave me; some manuscripts have By the power of your name I have kept safe those you have given me.
The man who was bound to be lost: Judas Iscariot, the traitor.
The scripture: see 13.18; Acts 1.20.

17.15   The Evil One: the Devil (see 12.31).

18.1   Kidron Brook: on the east side of Jerusalem, between the city and the Mount of Olives.

18.3   Temple guards: see 7.32.
Chief priests: see 7.32.
Pharisees: see 1.24.

18.5   Jesus of Nazareth: frequently a person was identified by the place he was from; for example, Elijah of Tishbe (1 Kgs 17.1); Joseph of Arimathea (Mark 15.43); Saul of Tarsus (Acts 9.11).

18.9   What he had said: see 17.12.

18.10   High Priest: see 11.49.

18.12   Jewish guards: see 7.32.

18.13   Annas: he had been High Priest from about A.D. 6 to 15.

18.14   Who had advised: see 11.50.

18.20   Synagogues: see 6.59.

18.28   Ritually clean: entering a Gentile residence would have made them ritually unclean.
Passover: see 2.13.

18.29   Pilate: Pontius Pilate, Roman governor of Judea, Samaria, and Idumea, A.D. 26-36.

18.32   The kind of death: the Jewish method of execution was stoning; the Roman method was crucifixion.

18.35   Chief priests: see 7.32.

18.37   You say that I am a king; or Yes I am, as you say.

18.39   Passover: see 2.13.

18.40   bandit; or insurrectionist.

19.6   Chief priests and the temple guards: see 7.32.

19.7   A law: see Lev 24.16.

19.11   The man: the High Priest.

19.13   sat down; or sat him down.

19.14   Passover: see 2.13.

19.17   Cross: here the horizontal beam which the condemned man was
        forced to carry to the place of execution.

19.21   Chief priests: see 7.32.

19.23   Robe: a short-sleeved knee-length garment that was worn next to
        the body.

19.24   The scripture: see Psa 22.18.

19.25   Magdalene: from Magdala, a town on the west side of Lake Galilee.

19.28   I am thirsty: see Psa 69.21.

19.29   Hyssop: a small bushy plant which was used in ceremonies of
        sprinkling.

19.31   Break the legs: in order to hasten death.
        Especially holy: because it was also Passover day.

19.35   believe; some manuscripts have continue to believe.

19.36   The scripture: see Num 9.12; Psa 34.20.

19.37   Another scripture: see Zech 12.10.

19.38   Arimathea: some 35 kilometers northwest of Jerusalem.

19.39   Myrrh: a perfume made from the hardened sap of a tree.
        Aloes: a sweet-smelling substance made from a plant.

19.42   Sabbath: see 5.9.

20.1   Magdalene: see 19.25.

20.21   Peace be with you: the customary greeting.

20.31 believe; some manuscripts have continue to believe.
Messiah: see 1.20.

21.1 Lake Tiberias: another name of Lake Galilee (see 6.1).
Cana: see 2.1.

21.15 more than these others do; or more than you love these others;
or more than you love these things.

21.19 The way in which Peter would die: that is, by execution.

21.20 That other disciple: see 13.23-25.

ACTS

1.1 Theophilus: see Luke 1.1.
First book: the Gospel according to Luke (see Luke 1.1-4).

1.2 Apostles: men who were commissioned to speak and act with the
authority of the one who sent them.

1.3 Kingdom of God: God's rule over mankind and the world.

1.4 when they came together; or while he was staying with them; or
while he was eating with them.
The gift my Father promised: the Holy Spirit (see 2.33).

1.5 John baptized with water: see Luke 3.16.

1.8 Judea and Samaria: two of the provinces into which Palestine
was then divided.

1.10 Two men dressed in white: the customary description of angels.

1.12 Mount of Olives: just to the east of Jerusalem, across Kidron
Valley.

1.16 Judas...the guide: see Luke 22.47.

1.18 The money: see Luke 22.3-6.
fell to his death; or swelled up.

1.19 Their own language: Aramaic.

1.20 The book of Psalms: see Psa 69.25; 109.8.

2.1 Pentecost: the Jewish festival of wheat harvest, on the 6th day
of Sivan (around May 20). The name "Pentecost" (meaning "fiftieth")
comes from the fact that the festival was held fifty days after
Passover.

2.5   Every country: at that time the Jews were widely scattered throughout different countries and in various provinces of the Roman Empire, some of which are named in verses 9-11.

2.16-20 The prophet Joel: see Septuagint Joel 2.28-32; the words "in the last days" are not part of the Old Testament passage.

2.17   Visions...dreams: means by which God would reveal his will to people.

2.18   Prophesy: to proclaim God's message.

2.22   Jesus of Nazareth: frequently a person was identified by the place he was from; for example, Elijah of Tishbe (1 Kgs 17.1); Joseph of Arimathea (Mark 15.43); Saul of Tarsus (Acts 9.11).

2.23   Sinful men: pagans (in this case the Romans), people who did not have God's Law.

2.25-28 David said: see Septuagint Psa 16.8-11.

2.27   The world of the dead: it was thought of as a vast abyss in the depths of the earth.

2.29   His grave: King David was buried in Jerusalem (see 1 Kgs 2.10).

2.30   Prophet: here the reference is to David's prediction (verse 31) of the resurrection of the Messiah.
God had promised him: see Psa 132.11.

2.31   David...said: see Psa 16.10.
Messiah: the title (the same as Christ) of the promised Savior whose coming was foretold by the Hebrew prophets.

2.33   to the right side; or by the authority.
Right side: the place of honor and authority.

2.34-35 David...said: see Psa 110.1.

2.35   A footstool under your feet: a figure of defeat and humiliation.

2.39   All who are far away: the Gentiles, as contrasted with the Jews.

2.42   Fellowship meals: probably meals which included a celebration of the Lord's Supper.

3.1   The hour for prayer: 3:00 P.M., the regular hour of the afternoon sacrifices in the Temple.

3.2   Beautiful Gate: perhaps at the east entrance of the Temple.

3.6   Jesus Christ of Nazareth: see 2.22.

3.11   Solomon's Porch: a colonnade on the east side of the Temple.

3.13   Servant: a messianic title, derived from such passages as
Isa 42.1; 52.13.
    Pilate: Pontius Pilate, the Roman governor of Judea, Samaria,
and Idumea, A.D. 26-36.

3.18   Messiah: see 2.31.

3.21   Prophets: God's messengers who proclaimed his message to the
people of Israel.

3.22-23 Moses said: see Septuagint Deut 18.15,18.

3.22   just as he sent me; or like me.

3.25   God...said: see Gen 22.18; 26.4.

4.1   priests; some manuscripts have chief priests.

4.5   Elders: respected Jewish religious leaders, some of whom were
members of the Supreme Council.
    Teachers of the Law: professionals who interpreted the Old
Testament, particularly the first five books.

4.6   High Priest: the priest who occupied the highest office in the
Jewish priestly system and who was president of the Supreme Council
of the Jews.
    Annas: the former High Priest, from about A.D. 6 to 15.
    Caiaphas: Annas' son-in-law, the High Priest A.D. 18-36.
    John; some manuscripts have Jonathan (who in A.D. 36 succeeded
Caiaphas as High Priest).

4.10   Jesus Christ of Nazareth: see 2.22.

4.11   The scripture: see Psa 118.22; the pronoun "you" is not in the
Old Testament passage.

4.13   Council: the supreme religious court of the Jews, composed of
about seventy leaders and presided over by the High Priest.

4.23   Chief priests: a group composed of the High Priest, former High
Priests still living, and the members of important families from
which the High Priests were chosen.

4.25-26 David...said: see Septuagint Psa 2.1-2.

4.26   Messiah: see 2.31.

4.27   Herod: Herod Antipas, ruler of the provinces of Galilee and
Perea, 4 B.C.--A.D. 39 (see Luke 23.7-11).
    Pilate: see 3.13.
    Holy Servant: see 3.13.

4.36   Levite: a member of the priestly tribe of Levi, who had the duty of helping in the Temple services (see Num 3.1-13).

5.12   Solomon's Porch: see 3.11.

5.16   Evil spirits: spirits which were regarded as being able to dominate people. These spirits were called "unclean" because they caused certain bodily disorders or actions which made people ritually defiled and thus prevented them from taking part in public worship until their defilement had been removed.

5.17   High Priest: see 4.6.
Sadducees: a small Jewish group, composed largely of priests, who based their beliefs primarily on the first five books of the Hebrew Scriptures.

5.21   Elders: see 4.5.
Council: see 4.13.

5.24   Chief priests: see 4.23.
Temple guards: Levites whose duty it was to guard and maintain order in the Temple.

5.31   to his right side; or by his power.
Right side: see 2.33.

5.34   Pharisee: a member of a Jewish religious party which was strict in obeying the Law of Moses and other regulations which had been added to it through the centuries.
Teacher of the Law: see 4.5.

5.36   Theudas: nothing certain is known about a Theudas who appeared before Judas the Galilean.

5.37   Judas...the census: a revolutionary who attempted to stir up a popular uprising against the Roman occupation forces in A.D. 6.

5.42   about Jesus the Messiah; or that the Messiah was Jesus.

6.1   Greek-speaking Jews: Jews whose place of origin was outside Palestine.
Native Jews: Jews whose home was in Palestine.

6.9   Synagogue: the public meeting house where Jews gathered on the Sabbath for worship.
Freedmen: Jews who had been slaves, but had bought or been given their freedom.

6.12   Elders: see 4.5.
Teachers of the Law: see 4.5.
Council: see 4.13.

6.14   Jesus of Nazareth: see 2.22.

7.3   God...said: see Gen 12.1.

7.6-7   God said: see Gen 15.13-14.

7.8   Circumcision: the ritual of removing the foreskin of a Jewish baby boy as a sign of God's covenant with the people of Israel (see Gen 17.9-14).

7.14   Seventy-five: this number is according to the Septuagint; the Hebrew text gives seventy (Gen 46.27; Exo 1.5).

7.30-34 Burning bush: see Exo 3.1-10.

7.37   just as he sent me; or like me.

7.40   They said: see Exo 32.1,23.

7.42   Stars: it was believed that the stars were ruled by spiritual powers.
       The book of the prophets: the section of the Old Testament that included the books of the twelve so-called "Minor Prophets" (from Hosea to Malachi).

7.42-43 It is written: see Septuagint Amos 5.25-27; "Babylon" replaces "Damascus" of the Old Testament passage.

7.43   Molech: the god of the Ammonites, a people who lived on the east side of the Jordan River.
       Rephan: an ancient god that was worshiped as the ruler of the planet Saturn.

7.44   Covenant Tent: see Exo 36.8-38.

7.46   the God of Jacob; some manuscripts have the people of Israel.

7.48-50 The prophet says: see Isa 66.1-2.

7.52   Servant: see 3.13.

7.53   Angels: according to a Jewish tradition, God had given the Law by means of angels (see Gal 3.19; Heb 2.2; Septuagint Deut 33.2).

7.56   Son of Man: a title of dignity, used only of Jesus in the New Testament.

7.58   Saul: the Hebrew name of the apostle Paul (see 13.9).

8.5   Philip: one of the seven helpers chosen by the church in Jerusalem (see 6.5).
       the principal city; some manuscripts have a city.
       Samaria: the province between Judea and Galilee. There was much hostility between Jews and Samaritans because of differences in race, customs, politics, and religion.

(71)

Messiah: see 2.31.

8.7   Evil spirits: see 5.16.

8.12   Kingdom of God: see 1.3.

8.26   south; or at midday.
          Gaza: a town about 85 kilometers southwest of Jerusalem, near
          the Mediterranean Sea.
          This road is not used nowadays; or This is the desert road.

8.27-28   Eunuch: a man physically incapable of having normal sexual
          relations; in ancient times such men often became influential
          officials in royal courts.
          To worship God: an indication that he was a convert to Judaism.

8.32-33   Passage of scripture: see Septuagint Isa 53.7-8.

8.36   Some manuscripts add verse 37: Philip said to him, "You may be
          baptized if you believe with all your heart." "I do," he answered;
          "I believe that Jesus Christ is the Son of God."

8.40   Azotus: north of Gaza, on the Mediterranean coast; Caesarea:
          farther north, on the coast.

9.1   High Priest: see 4.6.

9.2   Synagogues: see 6.9.
          Damascus: the most important city in Syria.
          The Way of the Lord: the Christian faith.

9.14   Chief priests: see 4.23.

9.20   Synagogues: see 6.9.

9.21   Chief priests: see 4.23.

9.27   Barnabas: see 4.36-37.

9.29   Greek-speaking Jews: see 6.1.

9.30   Tarsus: Saul's hometown (see 21.39), the capital of the Roman
          province of Cilicia.

9.32   Lydda: a town some 32 kilometers northwest of Jerusalem, and
          about 15 kilometers from Joppa.

9.35   Sharon: the coastal plain extending some 48 kilometers along
          the Mediterranean Sea, from Joppa north to Caesarea.

9.36   Joppa: a town on the Mediterranean Sea, about 15 kilometers
          northwest of Lydda.

Tabitha...Dorcas: the Aramaic and the Greek forms of the name; both mean "a deer."

10.2　　Worshiped God: in Acts this expression is used of Gentiles who worshiped the God of the Jews, attended the synagogue services, but were not full converts to Judaism.

10.3　　Three o'clock...afternoon: the regular Jewish hour for prayer (see 3.1).

10.6　　The sea: the Mediterranean.

10.14　　Ritually unclean: Old Testament laws prohibited the eating of certain birds and animals as being ritually unclean (see Lev 11).

10.19　　Three; some manuscripts have Some; one manuscript has Two.

10.30　　praying; some manuscripts have praying and fasting.
A man dressed in shining clothes: the customary description of an angel.

10.38　　Jesus of Nazareth: see 2.22.
Devil: the ruler of the forces of evil; the name means "the accuser."

10.43　　Prophets: see 3.21.

10.45　　Jewish believers...from Joppa: see 11.12.

10.46　　Strange tongues: not an intelligible language but strange sounds and utterances produced by a deep emotional and spiritual experience.

11.2　　Circumcising: see 7.8.

11.11　　I was; some manuscripts have we were.

11.12　　Six fellow believers from Joppa: see 10.45.

11.16　　The Lord had said: see 1.5.

11.20　　Antioch: the capital of the Roman province of Syria, the third greatest city in the Roman Empire (after Rome and Alexandria).
Gentiles; some manuscripts have Greek-speaking Jews or Greek-speaking people.

11.27　　Prophets: see 2.18. This is the first mention of Christian prophets in the New Testament.

11.28　　Claudius: Roman emperor A.D. 41-54; the famine occurred probably in A.D. 46.

11.30　　Church elders: officers who had general responsibility for the work of the church.

12.1   King Herod: Herod Agrippa I, grandson of Herod the Great and ruler of all Israel A.D. 41-44.

12.2   James: son of Zebedee and one of the twelve disciples of Jesus.

12.3   Festival of Unleavened Bread: a festival celebrating the deliverance of the ancient Hebrews from their slavery in Egypt; it was held Nisan 15-22 (around the beginning of April), and its name came from the practice of not using leaven (yeast) in making bread during that week.

12.4   Passover: the festival which was held on Nisan 14 (around the first of April), celebrating, as did the Festival of Unleavened Bread, the deliverance of the ancient Hebrews from their slavery in Egypt. The two festivals were celebrated as one.

12.15   His angel: according to Jewish belief, every person had an angel to watch over him (see Matt 18.10).

12.17   James: a brother of Jesus and one of the leaders of the church in Jerusalem (see Gal 1.19).

12.20   Tyre and Sidon: Gentile cities on the Mediterranean coast, north of Galilee.

12.25   from; some manuscripts have to.

13.1   Prophets: see 11.27.
        Herod: Herod Antipas, ruler of Galilee (see Luke 3.1).

13.3   Fasted: abstained temporarily from food as a religious duty.

13.4   Barnabas and Saul went: here begins Paul's first missionary tour, which ends with his return to Antioch (14.27-28).
        Seleucia: the seaport of Antioch, on the Mediterranean, about 20 kilometers away.
        Cyprus: where Barnabas was from (see 4.36).

13.5   Synagogues: see 6.9.

13.6   Paphos: the capital of Cyprus, on the west coast of the island.

13.7   Governor: the Roman official in charge of Cyprus, appointed by the Roman Senate.

13.9   Saul...Paul: his Hebrew and Roman names; it was common for Jews at that time to have both a Hebrew and a Roman name.

13.10   Devil: see 10.38.

13.14   Sabbath: the seventh day of the Jewish week, the holy day on which no work was allowed and when Jews had regular worship services in the synagogues.

13.15   Law of Moses: the first five books of the Hebrew Scriptures.
         Writings of the prophets: the second major division of the
Hebrew Scriptures.

13.16   Worship God: see 10.2.

13.18   he endured; some manuscripts have he took care of.

13.19   Seven nations: see Deut 7.1.

13.20   All of this took about 450 years. After this; or Some 450 years
         later.

13.22   God said: see Psa 89.20; 1 Sam 13.14.

13.25   John...said: see Luke 3.16.
         Take his sandals off: a menial task performed by a servant.

13.26   us; some manuscripts have you.

13.28   Pilate: see 3.13.

13.33   for us, who are their descendants; some manuscripts have for
         our descendants; other manuscripts have for their descendants.
         The second Psalm: see Psa 2.7.

13.34   God said: see Septuagint Isa 55.3.

13.35   Another passage: see Septuagint Psa 16.10.

13.40   Some manuscripts omit to you.

13.40-41 The prophets said: see Septuagint Hab 1.5.

13.47   The commandment: see Isa 49.6.

13.50   Worshiped God: see 10.2.

13.51   Shook the dust off their feet: a sign of complete rejection.

14.1   Synagogue: see 6.9.

14.11   Lycaonian: Barnabas and Paul could not understand this regional
         language; the common language was Greek.

14.12   Zeus: the supreme god of the Greeks (the same as the Roman
         Jupiter).
         Hermes: the Greek god who was the messenger of the gods (the
         same as the Roman Mercury).

14.22   Kingdom of God: see 1.3.

14.23   Elders: see 11.30.
        Fasting: see 13.3.

15.1   Circumcised: see 7.8.

15.2   Apostles: the original disciples of Jesus.
        Elders: see 11.30.

15.5   Pharisees: see 5.34.

15.13   James: see 12.17.

15.15-18 The scripture: see Septuagint Amos 9.11-12; Isa 45.21.

15.20   Strangled: in Jewish practice animals had to be killed in such
        a way as to drain out all the blood.
        Blood: Jewish law prohibited using blood as food (see Lev
        17.10-14).

15.21   Synagogues: see 6.9.
        Sabbath: see 13.14.

15.32   Prophets: see 11.27.

15.33   Some manuscripts add verse 34: But Silas decided to stay there.

15.38   Had turned back: see 13.13.

15.40   Left: here begins Paul's second missionary tour, which ends
        with his return to Antioch (18.22-23).

16.3   Circumcised: see 7.8. As the son of a Jewish mother (see
        verse 1), Timothy would be considered a Jew; but unless he were
        circumcised, he would not have been able to help Paul in the
        synagogues.

16.8   traveled right on through; or passed by.
        Troas: the port city of the province of Mysia, on the Aegean
        Sea.

16.9   Macedonia: a Roman province, covering what is now the northern
        half of Greece; its capital city was Thessalonica (see 17.1-10).

16.10   We got ready: here in Troas the author of Acts is present with
        Paul and stays with him as far as Philippi.

16.12   a city of the first district of Macedonia; some manuscripts
        have a leading city of the district of Macedonia or a leading city
        in that district in Macedonia.

16.13   Sabbath: see 13.14.

16.14   Who worshiped God: see 10.2.

16.37   Roman citizens: it was against Roman law to whip a citizen.

17.1   Synagogue: see 6.9.

17.2   Sabbaths: see 13.14.

17.3   Messiah: see 2.31.

17.14   The coast: to a port on the Aegean Sea, where he would board
         a ship and sail to Athens.

17.17   Synagogue: see 6.9.
         Worshiped God: see 10.2.

17.18   Epicurean...teachers: the Greek philosopher Epicurus (died 270
         B.C.) had taught that happiness is the highest good in life.
             Stoic teachers: they explained the teachings of the Greek
         philosopher Zeno (died 265 B.C.), who taught that happiness is
         found in not being affected by pleasure or by pain, by success
         or by failure.
             Jesus and the resurrection: in Greek the feminine noun
         "resurrection" (anastasis) could be understood to be the name of
         a goddess.

17.19   Areopagus: "the hill of Ares," the Greek god of war (the same
         as the Roman god Mars). The council of Athens originally met on
         the hill, and so was named for it.
             before the city council, the Areopagus; or to Mars' Hill.

17.22   in front of the city council; or on top of Mars' Hill.

17.24   An altar: in addition to altars dedicated to all known gods,
         altars were also dedicated to unknown gods, in case any of them
         had been overlooked.

17.26   one man; some manuscripts have one race.

17.28   Someone: probably the Cretan poet Epimenides (of the 6th century
         B.C.).
             Poets: probably Aratus, Greek poet, or Cleanthes, a Stoic
         philosopher (both of the 3rd century B.C.).

18.2   Claudius: see 11.28; he expelled the Jews from Rome around
         A.D. 49.

18.4   Synagogue: see 6.9.

18.5   Macedonia: specifically the city of Berea (see 17.14-15).
         Messiah: see 2.31.

18.6   <u>Shaking the dust from his clothes</u>: a sign of rejection (see 13.51).

18.7   <u>Worshiped God</u>: see 10.2.

18.12   <u>Gallio</u>: appointed governor in A.D. 51 of the Roman province of Achaia, which covered what is now the southern half of Greece; its capital was Corinth.

18.18   <u>Cenchreae</u>: the port city, on the Aegean Sea, of the city of Corinth.
<u>A vow he had taken</u>: a reference to the Jewish custom of shaving one's head as a sign that a vow had been kept.

18.19   <u>Synagogue</u>: see 6.9.

18.22   he went to Jerusalem and greeted; <u>or</u> he went and greeted.

18.23   <u>He left</u>: here begins Paul's third missionary tour, which ends with his return to Jerusalem (21.15).

18.25   <u>Way of the Lord</u>: see 9.2.
<u>Only the baptism of John</u>: indicating that he did not know Christian baptism (see 19.2-5).

19.1   <u>The province</u>: the Roman province of Asia, of which Ephesus was the capital city.

19.6   <u>Strange tongues</u>: see 10.46.

19.8   <u>Kingdom of God</u>: see 1.3.

19.9   <u>Way of the Lord</u>: see 9.2.
<u>Some manuscripts add</u> from 11:00 a.m. until 4:00 p.m.

19.12   <u>Evil spirits</u>: see 5.16.

19.14   <u>High Priest</u>: see 4.6.

19.19   <u>Silver coins</u>: a silver coin was the daily wage of a rural worker (see Matt 20.2).

19.20   In this powerful way the word of the Lord; <u>or</u> And so, by the power of the Lord, the message.

19.21   Paul made up his mind; <u>or</u> Paul, led by the Spirit, decided.
<u>Macedonia</u>: see 16.9.
<u>Achaia</u>: see 18.12.

19.22   <u>Asia</u>: see 19.1.

19.23   <u>Way of the Lord</u>: see 9.2.

19.24   Artemis: the Greek name (the Roman name was Diana) of Ephesus' chief goddess.

19.35   Sacred stone: perhaps a meteorite.

20.1   Macedonia: see 16.9.

20.2   Achaia: see 18.12.

20.5   Us: here again (see 16.10) the auther of Acts is present with Paul and continues with him to Rome (see 28.16).

20.6   From Philippi: that is, from its port city Neapolis (see 16.11). Festival of Unleavened Bread: see 12.3.

20.7   Saturday; or Sunday.
Fellowship meal: see 2.42.

20.15   Samos, and; some manuscripts add after stopping at Trogyllum.

20.16   Pentecost: see 2.1.

20.17   Elders: see 11.30.

20.25   Kingdom of God: see 1.3.

20.28   God; some manuscripts have the Lord.
the sacrificial death of his Son; or his own sacrificial death.

20.35   The words that the Lord Jesus himself said: this saying is not recorded in the Gospels.

21.1   Patara; some manuscripts add and Myra.

21.8   The seven men: see 6.1-6.

21.10   Agabus: see 11.28.

21.11   The Gentiles: the Roman authorities.

21.16   and took us to the house of the man we were going to stay with; or bringing with them the man at whose house we were going to stay.

21.18   James: see 12.17.
Elders: see 11.30.

21.21   Circumcise: see 7.8.

21.24   Shave their heads: see 18.18.

21.25   Letter: see 15.23-29.

21.28   Brought some Gentiles into the Temple: whoever took a Gentile into the Temple precincts beyond the court of the Gentiles could be put to death; there was a written notice to this effect on the wall separating the court of the Gentiles from the inner areas of the Temple.

21.34   The fort: the Antonia Fort, at the northwest corner of the Temple area, where the Roman troops were garrisoned.

21.35   Steps: two flights of steps led up from the Temple area to the fort.

21.38   Armed terrorists: extreme nationalists who sought to free Israel from the Romans. The Jewish historian Josephus reports that this revolt took place in A.D. 54.

22.3   Gamaliel: see 5.34.

22.4   Way: see 9.2.

22.5   High Priest: see 4.6.
        Council: see 4.13.

22.8   Jesus of Nazareth: see 2.22.

22.14   Servant: see 3.13.

22.20   Stephen: see 7.57-60.

22.25   to be whipped; or with ropes.
        Roman citizen: see 16.37.

22.30   Chief priests: see 4.23.
        Council: see 4.13.

23.2   Ananias: High Priest from about A.D. 47 to 59.

23.5   The scripture: see Exo 22.28.

23.6   Sadducees: a small Jewish group, composed largely of priests, who based their beliefs primarily on the first five books of the Hebrew Scriptures.
        Pharisees: see 5.34.

23.9   Teachers of the Law: see 4.5.

23.10   Fort: see 21.34.

23.14   Chief priests: see 4.23.
        Elders: see 4.5.

23.15   Council: see 4.13.

23.23   Caesarea: on the Mediterranean Sea, some 90 kilometers north-west of Jerusalem; it was the chief city of Palestine and the official residence of the Roman governor.

23.24   Felix: Roman governor of Judea A.D. 52-60.

23.30   Some manuscripts add With best wishes.

23.31   Antipatris: a town about 60 kilometers northwest of Jerusalem.

23.32   Fort: see 21.34.

24.1   Elders: see 4.5.

24.5   Party: outsiders considered the Christian religion to be a sect of Judaism; "Nazarenes" means "from Nazareth" (see 2.22).

24.6   Some manuscripts add verses 6b-8a: We planned to judge him according to our own Law, 7but the commander Lysias came, and with great violence took him from us. 8Then Lysias gave orders that his accusers should come before you.

24.12   Synagogues: see 6.9.

24.14   Way: see 9.2.
         Law of Moses and the books of the prophets: see 13.15.

24.24   Drusilla: sister of Herod Agrippa II and of Bernice (see 25.13).

24.27   Porcius Festus: Roman governor of Judea A.D. 60-62.

25.1   arrived in the province; or took office.
         Province: Judea.
         Caesarea: see 23.23.

25.2   Chief priests: see 4.23.

25.11   Appeal to the Emperor: a Roman citizen had the right to demand that his case be decided by the Emperor in Rome; at this time the Emperor was Nero, who ruled A.D. 54-68.

25.13   King Agrippa: Herod Agrippa II, king of Chalcis, a small country north of Palestine, and ruler of other nearby territories; he and Bernice were children of Herod Agrippa I (see 12.1).

25.15   Chief priests: see 4.23.
         Elders: see 4.5.

26.4   My own country: the province of Cilicia, of which Tarsus was the capital (see 22.3).

26.5   Pharisees: see 5.34.

26.6   The hope I have: in the resurrection (see 23.6; 24.15).

26.11   Synagogues: see 6.9.

26.17   Some manuscripts omit of me.

26.18   Satan: another name for the Devil; it means "the opponent."

26.23   Messiah: see 2.31.

26.28   In this short time; or With such little effort.

27.1   We: see 20.5.

27.9   Day of Atonement: this was celebrated toward the end of September or beginning of October, at which time bad weather made sailing dangerous.

27.12   southwest and northwest; or northeast and southeast.

27.37   276; some manuscripts have 275; others have about 76.

28.10   They gave us many gifts; or They paid us many honors.

28.11   "The Twin Gods": Castor and Pollux, twin sons of Zeus, gods worshiped by sailors.

28.15   Market of Appius: a town about 70 kilometers south of Rome. Three Inns: a town about 55 kilometers south of Rome.

28.20   Him for whom the people of Israel hope: the Messiah.

28.22   Party: see 24.5.

28.23   Kingdom of God: see 1.3.
Law of Moses and the writings of the prophets: see 13.15.

28.26-27   He said: see Septuagint Isa 6.9-10.

28.29   Some manuscripts add verse 29: After Paul said this, the Jews left, arguing violently among themselves.

ROMANS

1.1   Apostle: one who is commissioned to speak and act with the authority of the one who sent him.

1.2   The Holy Scriptures: the Hebrew Bible, the Old Testament.

1.4   as to his divine holiness; or because of his spirit of holiness; or because of the Holy Spirit.
by being raised; or when he was raised.

1.17   The scripture: see Hab 2.4.
put right with God through faith shall live; or put right with
God shall live through faith.

1.25   the truth about God for a lie; or the true God for a false one.

1.30   are hateful to God, insolent; or hate God, and are insolent.

2.1   My friend: in this section (2.1-11) Paul is addressing his
Jewish readers.

2.4   God is kind, because he is trying; or God's kindness is trying.

2.5   The Day: the final Day of Judgment.

2.18   choose; or judge.

2.24   The scripture: see Septuagint Isa 52.5.

2.25   Circumcision: the rite of cutting off the foreskin of a Jewish
baby boy as a sign of God's covenant with the people of Israel
(see Gen 17.9-14).

3.2   message; or revelation.

3.4   The scripture: see Septuagint Psa 51.4.

3.9   any better condition than the Gentiles? Not at all!; or any
worse condition than the Gentiles? Not altogether.

3.10-18   The Scriptures: see Septuagint Psa 14.1-3; Septuagint Psa 5.9;
Septuagint Psa 140.3; Septuagint Psa 10.7; Isa 59.7-8; Psa 36.1.

3.21   The Law of Moses and the prophets: respectively, the first five
books of the Hebrew Scriptures and the second division of the
Hebrew Scriptures. The phrase was often used to refer to the whole
Hebrew Bible.

4.1   Some manuscripts omit What was his experience?

4.3   The scripture: see Gen 15.6.

4.6-8   David...spoke: see Psa 32.1-2.

4.17   The scripture: see Gen 17.5.

4.18   The scripture: see Gen 15.5.

5.1   we have; some manuscripts have let us have.

5.2   Some manuscripts omit by faith.
we boast; or let us boast.

5.3   We also boast; or Let us also boast.

(83)

5.12   One man: Adam.

5.14   The one who was to come: Christ.

7.2   is bound by the law to her husband as long as he lives; or as long as her husband lives, is bound to the law.

7.5   Human nature: this expression (a translation of the Greek word for "flesh") is often used in Paul's letters to mean man as he is, apart from God and subject to sin.

7.7   Do not desire: the tenth commandment (see Exo 20.17).

7.14   Spiritual: it was given by God and expressed his will for man. Mortal man: see 7.5.

8.2   me; some manuscripts have you; others have us.

8.3   to do away with sin; or as a sin offering.

8.4   Human nature: see 7.5.

8.10   the Spirit is life for you; or your spirit is alive.

8.18   The glory: the final manifestation of God's saving power.

8.20-21 Yet there was the hope that creation itself would; or Yet there was hope, because creation itself will.

8.23   Some manuscripts omit make us his sons and.

8.28   in all things God works for good with those who love him; some manuscripts have all things work for good for those who love God.

8.35   Christ; some manuscripts have God.

8.36   The scripture: see Psa 44.22.

8.39   The world above...the world below: probably evil spiritual forces in the heavens (see Eph 2.2) and in the depths of the earth.

9.4   Sons: see Exo 4.22; Jer 31.9; Hos 11.1.
        Covenants: with Noah (Gen 6.18; 9.9), Abraham (Gen 15.18; 17.2,7-9), the people of Israel (Exo 19.1-8). Some manuscripts have covenant.

9.5   May God, who rules over all; or And may he, who is God ruling over all.

9.7   God said: see Gen 21.12.

9.8   Children born in the usual way: a reference to the descendants
Abraham had through Ishmael, his son by Hagar (see Gal 4.22-23).
Children born as a result of God's promise: the descendants
Abraham had through Isaac (see Gen 17.19-21).

9.9   God's promise: see Gen 18.10.
At the right time; or At this time next year.

9.11-12   God said: see Gen 25.23.

9.13   The scripture: see Mal 1.2-3.

9.15   He said: see Exo 33.19.

9.17   The scripture: see Septuagint Exo 9.16.

9.25-26   He says: see Hos 2.23; 1.10.

9.27-28   Isaiah exclaims: see Septuagint Isa 10.22-23.

9.29   Isaiah had said: see Septuagint Isa 1.9.
Sodom and Gomorrah: see Gen 19.24-25.

9.33   The scripture: see Septuagint Isa 28.16; 8.14.
In him: the one called "a stone...a rock"; here the reference
is to Christ (see 1 Peter 2.4-8).

10.5   Moses wrote: see Lev 18.5.

10.6-8   The scripture: see Deut 30.12-14.

10.7   The world below: the world of the dead.

10.11   The scripture: see Septuagint Isa 28.16.

10.13   The scripture: see Joel 2.32.

10.15   The scripture: see Isa 52.7.

10.16   Isaiah...said: see Septuagint Isa 53.1.

10.18   The scripture: see Septuagint Psa 19.4.

10.19   Moses...answer: see Deut 32.21.

10.20   Isaiah...says: see Isa 65.1.

10.21   He says: see Septuagint Isa 65.2.

11.2-3   The scripture: see 1 Kgs 19.10.

11.4   Answer: see 1 Kgs 19.18.
Baal: a god worshiped by the Canaanites.

11.8   The scripture: see Deut 29.4; Isa 29.10.

11.9-10 David says: see Septuagint Psa 69.22-23.

11.26-27 The scripture: see Septuagint Isa 59.20-21; 27.9.
         Zion: the city of Jerusalem.

11.31   Some manuscripts omit the second now.

11.34-35 The scripture: see Septuagint Isa 40.13; Job 41.11.

12.16   accept humble duties; or make friends with humble people.

12.19   The scripture: see Deut 32.35.

12.20   The scripture: see Septuagint Prov 25.21-22.

13.9   The commandments: see Exo 20.13-15,17.
         The one command: see Lev 19.18.

13.12   Day: the time of the final and complete redemption by Christ.

14.11   The scripture: see Septuagint Isa 49.18; 45.23.

14.19   we must always aim; some manuscripts have we always aim.

14.21   Some manuscripts add or commit sin or become weak.

14.23   Some manuscripts add here what appears in 16.25-27.

15.3   The scripture: see Psa 69.9.

15.4   The Scriptures: see 1.2.

15.7   you; some manuscripts have us.

15.9   The scripture: see Psa 18.49.

15.10   It says: see Deut 32.43.

15.11   Again: see Psa 117.1.

15.12   Isaiah says: see Septuagint Isa 11.10.
         Jesse: the father of King David, the ancestor of Jesus.

15.19   Illyricum: a Roman province on the coast of the Adriatic Sea,
         in what is now Yugoslavia.

15.21   The scripture: see Septuagint Isa 52.15.

15.23   I have finished my work: Paul saw his task as that of a pioneer,
         proclaiming the gospel in places which had not been reached by others.
         These regions: perhaps Corinth, capital of the Roman province of
         Achaia.

15.26   Macedonia and Achaia: two Roman provinces corresponding to what are now the northern half and the southern half of Greece.
An offering: see 1 Cor 16.1-4; 2 Cor 8.1-4; 9.1-5; Gal 2.10.

15.29   of Christ; some manuscripts have of the Good News about Christ.

15.33   One old manuscript omits Amen and adds what appears in 16.25-27.

16.1   who serves; or who is a deaconess of.
Cenchreae: the eastern port city of Corinth.

16.5   The province of Asia: a Roman province in what is now Turkey; its capital city was Ephesus.

16.7   Junias; or June; some manuscripts have Julia.
The apostles: either the twelve men chosen by Jesus or else other Christian leaders who were sent out by the churches (see 1.1).

16.20   Satan: the ruler of the forces of evil; the name means "the opponent."
Some manuscripts omit the second sentence of this verse.

16.22   Tertius, the writer: a man serving as Paul's secretary, who wrote down what Paul dictated.

16.23   Some manuscripts add verse 24: The grace of our Lord Jesus Christ be with you all. Amen. Other manuscripts add this after 16.27.

16.26   The writings of the prophets: the Old Testament Scriptures.

16.27   Some manuscripts have verses 25-27 here and after 14.23; others have them only after 14.23; others omit them; one manuscript has them after 15.33.

1 CORINTHIANS

1.1   Apostle: one who is commissioned to speak and act with the authority of the one who sent him.
Sosthenes: perhaps the man referred to in Acts 18.17.

1.4   my God; some manuscripts have God.

1.8   The Day of our Lord: the final day of Judgment, when all will be judged by God and Christ.

1.12   Apollos: a Christian leader who had preached the gospel in Corinth (see Acts 18.24--19.1).

1.13   Christ has been divided; some manuscripts have Christ cannot be divided.

1.14   I thank God; some manuscripts have I am thankful.
         Crispus: a convert from Judaism, who lived in Corinth (see
Acts 18.8).
         Gaius: probably the man named in Romans 16.23 as Paul's host
while he was in Corinth.

1.16   Stephanas: see 1 Cor 16.15-16.

1.19   The scripture: see Septuagint Isa 29.14.

1.31   The scripture: see Jer 9.24.

2.1   God's secret truth; some manuscripts have the testimony about
God.

2.6   The powers: the evil spiritual forces who now control the world
through those who obey them (see Eph 6.12; Col 1.16).

2.8   The Lord of glory: Christ, the revelation of God's nature and
power (see Heb 1.3).

2.9   The scripture: see Isa 64.4.

2.10   But; some manuscripts have For.

2.13   to those who have the Spirit; or with words given by the Spirit.

2.16   The scripture: see Septuagint Isa 40.13.

3.4   Apollos: see 1.12.

3.9   partners working together for God; or God's partners.

3.13   The Day: see 1.8.

3.19   The scripture: see Job 5.13.

3.20   Another scripture: see Psa 94.11.

4.6   Apollos: see 1.12.

4.9   Apostles: not just the twelve men chosen by Jesus but also
others (see Rom 16.7).

4.15   Guardians: at that time a guardian was a slave who took his
master's children to school and looked after them when they were
not in school.

4.17   Timothy: one of Paul's colleagues who traveled with him and
helped in the work (see Acts 19.22; Phil 2.19-22).

5.1   Stepmother: marriage between a man and his stepmother was prohibited by Roman law and the Jewish Scriptures (see Lev 18.8).

5.5   Satan: the ruler of the forces of evil; the name means "the opponent."
        Body destroyed: here the thought seems to be that the forces operating in the world of evil would bring about the sinner's death; his spirit, however, would be saved.
        The Day of the Lord: see 1.8.
        the Lord; some manuscripts have the Lord Jesus.

5.7   Yeast: a substance (leaven) which is added to flour to make the mass of dough rise before being baked; here, as elsewhere, yeast is a figure of sin which spreads and infects others.
        Passover: the Jewish festival which celebrated the deliverance of the ancient Hebrews from their slavery in Egypt; as part of the festival, all leavened bread was discarded and only bread made without leaven was eaten during the following week (see Exo 12.14-20).

5.9   The letter: one written before this one but which has not been preserved (unless, as some think, part of it is 2 Cor 6.14--7.1).

5.11   What I meant was; or But now I write.

5.13   The scripture: see Deut 17.7.

6.9   God's Kingdom: the blessings of God's rule, which he has in store for his people in the life to come.

6.16   The scripture: see Gen 2.24.

7.1   A man does well not to marry; or You say that a man does well not to marry.

7.10   The Lord's...command: see Mark 10.2-12.

7.14   Acceptable to God: because one parent is a believer, the children are accepted by God as the offspring of a Christian marriage.

7.15   you; some manuscripts have us.

7.16   How can you be sure...that you will not save; or How do you know...that you will save.

7.18   A circumcised man: a Jew.
        Circumcision: the rite of cutting off the foreskin of a Jewish baby boy as a sign of God's covenant with the people of Israel (see Gen 17.9-14).
        An uncircumcised man: a Gentile.

7.21   but if you have a chance to become a free man, use it; or but even if you have a chance to become a free man, choose rather to make the best of your condition as a slave.

7.26   The present distress: either troubles and persecutions or the end of the age (see verses 29,31).

7.36   an engaged couple...as he wants to; <u>or</u> a man and his unmarried daughter: if he feels that he is not acting properly toward her, and if she is at the right age to marry, then he should do as he wishes and let her get married.

7.37   not to marry; <u>or</u> not to let his daughter get married.

7.38   marries; <u>or</u> lets his daughter get married.
doesn't marry; <u>or</u> doesn't let her get married.

7.40   God's; <u>a few manuscripts have</u> Christ's.

8.1   <u>Food offered to idols</u>: much of the meat sold in market places had been previously offered to pagan gods in idol temples, and some Christians believed that they would be guilty of idolatry if they ate such meat.

9.1   <u>Apostle</u>: see 1.1.

9.4   <u>Be given food and drink</u>: that is, as payment by the churches he serves.

9.5   <u>The Lord's brothers</u>: see Mark 6.3.

9.6   <u>Barnabas</u>: an outstanding Christian leader, Paul's companion in the early years of his work (see Acts 4.36; 13.1--15.39; Gal 2.1).

9.9   <u>We read</u>: see Deut 25.4.

9.14   <u>The Lord has ordered</u>: see Matt 10.10; Luke 10.7.

10.1   <u>The cloud</u>: see Exo 13.21-22.
<u>The Red Sea</u>: see Exo 14.19-29.

10.3   <u>Spiritual bread</u>: the manna provided by God (see Exo 16.31-35).

10.4   <u>Spiritual drink</u>: the water provided by God (see Exo 17.3-6; Num 20.7-11).
<u>The spiritual rock that went with them</u>: according to Jewish popular tradition the rock from which the Israelites drank water on two separate occasions (see Exo 17.6; Num 20.7-11) was the same one and it followed them during their wanderings in the wilderness.

10.7   <u>The scripture</u>: see Exo 32.6.

10.8   <u>Sexual immorality</u>: see Num 25.1-9.

10.9   the Lord; <u>some manuscripts have</u> Christ.
<u>Killed by snakes</u>: see Num 21.5-6.

10.10   <u>They were destroyed</u>: see Num 16.41-49.

10.26   <u>The scripture</u>: see Psa 24.1

11.10   The angels: either good angels, who were considered to be responsible for order in public worship, or evil angels, who lusted after women.

11.21   Meal: at that time the Lord's Supper was celebrated at the close of a regular meal eaten in common by the worshipers; this meal became known as the love feast (agape).

12.10   Strange tongues: not an intelligible language but strange sounds and utterances produced by a deep emotional and spiritual experience.

12.28   Apostles...prophets: see Eph 4.11.

13.3   to be burned; some manuscripts have in order to boast.

13.8   Strange tongues: see 12.10.

13.12   Mirror: made of polished metal and so giving an imperfect reflection.

14.2   Strange tongues: see 12.10.

14.16   Amen: a Hebrew word meaning "So may it be."

14.21   The Scriptures: the Hebrew Bible, the Old Testament. It is written: see Isa 28.11-12.

14.38   pay no attention to him; or God pays no attention to him; some manuscripts have let him ignore it.

15.7   James: the brother of the Lord and leader in the Jerusalem church (see Acts 12.17; Gal 1.19).

15.8   whose birth was abnormal; or who was born at the wrong time. Birth: a figure of Paul's conversion to the Christian faith.

15.9   Apostles: see 4.9.

15.19   If our hope in Christ is good for this life only and no more; or If all we have in this life is our hope in Christ.

15.27   The scripture: see Psa 8.6.

15.29   Baptized for the dead: apparently in the Corinthian church there were people who were baptized to guarantee the resurrection of their unbaptized dead relatives or friends; no other reference to such a practice appears in the New Testament.

15.32   Wild beasts: probably not meant literally but figuratively of dangerous enemies. The saying: see Isa 22.13.

(91)

15.33   "Bad companions ruin good character": a proverb attributed to the Greek poet Menander (4th century B.C.).

15.45   The scripture: see Gen 2.7.
The last Adam: Jesus Christ.

15.49   we will wear; some manuscripts have let us wear.

15.50   God's Kingdom: see 6.9.

15.51   Die: that is, before the Lord comes.

15.54   The scripture: see Isa 25.8.

15.55   Where, Death: see Septuagint Hos 13.14.

16.1   Galatia: a Roman province in what is now Turkey.
The money to be raised: see Rom 15.25-28; 2 Cor 8.1-4; 9.1-5; Gal 2.10.

16.5   Macedonia: a Roman province corresponding to what is now northern Greece; its capital was Thessalonica.

16.8   Pentecost: the Jewish festival of wheat harvest on the 6th day of Sivan (around May 20). The name "Pentecost" (meaning "fiftieth") comes from the fact that the festival was held fifty days after Passover.

16.10   Timothy: see 4.17.

16.12   Appolos: see 1.12.
he is not completely convinced; or it is not at all God's will.

16.15   Achaia: a Roman province corresponding to what is now southern Greece; its capital city was Corinth.

16.19   Asia: a Roman province in what is now Turkey; its capital city was Ephesus.
Aquila and Priscilla: a Christian couple, close friends and companions of Paul (see Acts 18.1-19).

16.22   Our Lord, come!: the meaning of the Aramaic phrase Marana tha.

2 CORINTHIANS

1.1   Apostle: see 1 Cor 1.1.
Timothy: see 1 Cor 4.17.
Achaia: a Roman province corresponding to what is now southern Greece; its capital city was Corinth.

1.8   Asia: a Roman province in what is now Turkey; its capital city was Ephesus.

1.10   such terrible dangers of death; some manuscripts have terrible death.

1.12   frankness; some manuscripts have holiness.

1.14   The Day: see 1 Cor 1.8.

1.15   be blessed twice; some manuscripts have have a double pleasure.

1.16   Macedonia: a Roman province corresponding to what is now northern Greece; its capital city was Thessalonica. Other cities in the province which Paul had visited were Neapolis, Philippi, Amphipolis, Apollonia, and Berea.
        My trip to Judea: to take to the needy believers (especially in Jerusalem) an offering from the churches in which Paul himself worked (see 1 Cor 16.1).

1.19   Silas: a colleague and assistant of Paul (see Acts 15.22--18.5).

1.20   Amen: see 1 Cor 14.16.

2.3   That letter: written before this one but not preserved unless, as some think, part or all of it now appears as chapters 10-13 of 2 Cor (see also 2.9; 7.8,12).

2.11   Satan: the ruler of the forces of evil; the name means "the opponent."

2.12   Troas: a city on the Aegean Sea, in the western part of the Roman province of Asia.

2.13   Titus: a colleague and assistant of Paul (see Gal 2.1-3).
        Macedonia: see 1.16.

2.14   Victory procession: often a Roman general returning from a successful military campaign would parade with his troops through the streets of Rome, accompanied by his defeated enemies.

2.15   Incense: a substance which produced a sweet smell when burned; it was regularly used in connection with animal sacrifices in Hebrew worship.

3.2   our; some manuscripts have your.

3.6   Covenant: God's agreement with his people; here the new covenant effected by Jesus Christ (see 1 Cor 11.25) is contrasted with the old covenant, the Law of Moses.

3.7   The brightness on Moses' face: see Exo 34.29.

3.13   Moses...put on a veil: see Exo 34.33.

3.14   The books of the old covenant: the Hebrew Bible, the Old Testament.

(93)

3.16   <u>Verse 16 may be translated</u>: But the veil is removed whenever someone turns to the Lord.
<u>The scripture</u>: see Exo 34.34.

3.18   reflect; <u>or</u> gaze at.

4.4   <u>The evil god</u>: Satan (see 2.11).

4.6   <u>God...said</u>: see Gen 1.3.

4.13   <u>The scripture</u>: see Septuagint Psa 116.10.

5.14   <u>One man</u>: Christ.

5.16   <u>At one time</u>: before becoming a Christian.

5.17   he is a new being; <u>or</u> there is a new creation.

5.19   God was making all mankind his friends through Christ; <u>or</u> God was in Christ making all mankind his friends.

5.21   share our sin; <u>or</u> a sin offering.

6.2   <u>God says</u>: see Isa 49.8.

6.14--7.1   See note on 1 Cor 5.9.

6.16   <u>God...said</u>: see Lev 26.12; Ezek 37.27.

6.17-18   <u>The Lord says</u>: see Isa 52.11; 2 Sam 7.14.

7.2   Here the thought picks up from 6.13 (6.14--7.1 interrupts the sequence).

7.5   <u>Macedonia</u>: see 1.16.

7.6   <u>Titus</u>: see 2.13.

7.8   <u>That letter</u>: see 2.3.

7.12   <u>The one who did wrong</u>: the leader of the opposition to Paul in the church in Corinth (see 2.5-8).
<u>The one who was wronged</u>: Paul himself or one of his colleagues.

8.1   <u>Macedonia</u>: see 1.16.

8.4   <u>Helping God's people in Judea</u>: see 1.16.

8.7   your love for us; <u>some manuscripts have</u> our love for you.

8.9   <u>Rich as he was</u>: in his pre-incarnate state.
<u>He made himself poor</u>: in his incarnation (see Phil 2.6-8).

8.15   The scripture: see Exo 16.18.

8.18   The brother: it is not certain who this is.

8.22   Our brother: apparently someone other than the one referred to in verse 18 and, like him, also unidentified.

9.2   The people in Macedonia: that is, where Paul was as he wrote these words.
The brothers in Achaia: the Christians in Corinth, to whom Paul was writing.

9.3   These brothers: Titus (8.16-17) and the others who are unidentified (8.18,22).

9.9   The scripture: see Psa 112.9.

9.15   His priceless gift: salvation through his Son.

10.7   You are looking at the outward appearance of things; or Consider the plain facts.

10.16   Countries beyond you: to the west, probably including Spain (see Rom 15.23-38).

10.17   The scripture: see Jer 9.24.

11.3   Some manuscripts omit and pure.
Eve: see Gen 3.1-5,13.

11.5   So-called "apostles": Christian leaders who did not consider Paul to be a genuine apostle (see verses 12-13).

11.8   Other churches: in Macedonia (see 1.16).

11.9   The brothers...from Macedonia: especially from the church in Philippi (see Phil 4.10-20).

11.24   The thirty-nine lashes: the severest legal Jewish whipping was 39 lashes, one less than the maximum prescribed by the Law (see Deut 25.3).

11.32   King Aretas: king of Nabatea, a country southeast of Palestine; it appears that at that time Damascus, in Syria, was under his control.

11.33   Escaped: see Acts 9.23-25.

12.2   A certain Christian man: Paul himself.
The highest heaven: where God dwells.

12.7   A painful physical ailment: it is not known precisely what this was.

(95)

12.11   Very special "apostles" of yours: see 11.5.

12.18   The other Christian brother: see 8.18,22.

13.1   The scripture: see Deut 19.15.

13.13   fellowship of; or fellowship in.

GALATIANS

1.1   Apostle: one who is commissioned to speak and act with the authority of the one who sent him.

1.2   Galatia: a Roman province in what is now eastern Turkey; Paul had established Christian work in Antioch of Pisidia, Iconium, Lystra, and Derbe (see Acts 13.13--14.21).

1.6   by the grace of Christ; some manuscripts have by his grace.

1.17   Arabia: probably the kingdom of Nabatea, southeast of Palestine; its capital city was Petra.
         Damascus: the most important city in Syria.

1.19   any other apostle except James; or any other apostle; the only other person I saw was James.
         James, the Lord's brother: a leader of the church in Jerusalem (see Acts 15.13).

1.21   Cilicia: a Roman province in what is now southeast Turkey; its capital city was Tarsus, where Paul was born (Acts 22.3).

2.1   Fourteen years later: probably from the time of his conversion (1.15-16).
         Barnabas: an outstanding Christian leader, Paul's companion in the early years of his work (see Acts 4.36; 13.1--15.39).
         Titus: Paul's colleague and assistant.

2.9   James: see 1.19.
         Peter, and John: two of the twelve apostles.

2.10   The needy in their group: see Rom 15.26; 1 Cor 16.1-4; 2 Cor 8.1-4; 9.1-5.
         have; or had.

2.11   Antioch: in Syria (see Acts 11.19-26).

2.16   The Law: the Hebrew Scriptures, especially the Torah, the first five books.

3.1   Foolish: the Galatians are acting as if they had lost their senses.

3.6   The scripture: see Gen 15.6.

3.8   The scripture: see Gen 12.3.

3.10   The scripture: see Septuagint Deut 27.26.

3.11   The scripture: see Hab 2.4.
          put right with God through faith shall live; or put right with
          God shall live through faith.

3.12   The scripture: see Lev 18.5.

3.13   A curse for us: that is, the object of God's condemnation.
          The scripture: see Deut 21.23.

3.15   when two people agree...no one can break it; or after a will
          has been drawn up and certified, no one can annul it.

3.16   The scripture: see Gen 12.7.

3.17   Four hundred and thirty years later: the time from God's
          covenant with Abraham to the giving of the Law at Mount Sinai,
          according to Septuagint Exo 12.40.

3.19   Abraham's descendant: Christ (see verse 16).
          Angels: according to popular Jewish teaching, angels were
          present when the Law was given on Mount Sinai (see Septuagint
          Deut 33.2; Acts 7.38,53).
          A man: Moses.

3.20   and God is one; or and God acts alone.

3.22   The scripture: see Psa 14.3; Rom 3.9-18.

3.24   until Christ came; or to lead us to Christ.

4.3   The ruling spirits of the universe: the evil spiritual forces
          which rule the world (also verse 9); or the Greek phrase may mean
          elementary and worthless religious rules.
          Spiritual maturity: acceptance of Jesus as Messiah and Lord.

4.6   To show that you are; or Because you are.

4.13   Because I was sick: due to some unspecified illness Paul stayed
          in Galatia and preached the gospel there.

4.14   to you; some manuscripts have to me.

4.17   Those other people: Paul's opponents, who taught that Gentiles
          must first be circumcised before becoming Christians.

4.22   A slave woman: Hagar (see Gen 16.15).
          A free woman: Sarah (see Gen 21.2).

4.25   Hagar...is; some manuscripts have Sinai is a mountain in Arabia, and it is.
In slavery: to the Jewish Law.

4.27   The scripture: see Isa 54.1.

4.28   you; some manuscripts have we.

4.29   The son...born in the usual way: Ishmael, son of Hagar.
The one...born because of God's Spirit: Isaac, son of Sarah.

4.30   The scripture: Gen 21.10.

5.2   Circumcised: as a requirement for becoming Christian.

5.9   Yeast: a substance (leaven) which is added to flour to make the mass of dough rise before being baked; here, as elsewhere, yeast is a figure of sin which spreads and infects others.

5.14   One commandment: see Lev 19.18.

5.16   Human nature: this expression (a translation of the Greek word for "flesh") is often used in Paul's letters to mean man as he is, apart from God and subject to sin.

5.21   are envious; some manuscripts add commit murder.
The Kingdom of God: the blessings of God's rule, which he has in store for his people in the life to come.

6.2   you will obey; some manuscripts have obey.

6.17   The scars: as a result of the ill treatment that Paul had suffered because of his work as an apostle.

EPHESIANS

1.1   Apostle: see Gal 1.1.
Some manuscripts omit in Ephesus.
Ephesus: the capital city of the Roman province of Asia, in what is now western Turkey.

1.3   The heavenly world: a phrase appearing only in this letter (1.20; 2.6; 3.10; 6.12); it means the realm, apart from this physical universe, where spiritual events take place.

1.5   before him. Because of his love God; or before him and to live in love. God.

1.12   Us: Jewish Christians.
who were the first to hope; or who had already hoped.

1.13   You: Gentile Christians.

1.20   His right side: the place of honor and power (see Psa 110.1).

1.21   Rulers, authorities, powers, and lords: spiritual forces which control the universe.

1.23   who himself completes all things everywhere; or who is himself completely filled with God's fullness.

2.2   The ruler...the spirit: the Devil.

2.6   The heavenly world: see 1.3.

2.12   The covenants: with Noah (Gen 6.18; 9.9), Abraham (Gen 15.18; 17.2,7-9), the people of Israel (Exo 19.1-8).

2.20   the foundation laid by the apostles and prophets; or the foundation, that is, the apostles and prophets.
        Prophets: here a Christian group, referring to those who spoke in the name of the Lord Jesus (see Acts 13.1; 1 Cor 12.28-29).

3.5   Prophets: see 2.20.

3.10   Rulers and powers: see 1.21.
        The heavenly world: see 1.3.

3.13   I beg you, then, not to be discouraged; or I pray that I will not become discouraged.

3.15   Every family in heaven: the angels.

4.8   The scripture: see Psa 68.18.

4.9   the lowest depths of the earth; or the lower depths, the earth itself.
        The lowest depths of the earth: the world of the dead.

4.11   Apostles: primarily the twelve men chosen by Jesus, but including also others who, like Paul, had been directly commissioned by Christ.
        Prophets: see 2.20.
        Evangelists: those who went about proclaiming the gospel.
        Pastors and teachers: those who exercised the double function in a particular church.

4.30   The Day: the final day of Judgment.

5.9   the light; some manuscripts have the Spirit.

5.14   anything that is clearly revealed becomes light; or it is light that clearly reveals everything.
        It is said: the words that follow are probably part of an early Christian hymn.

5.26   Washing it in water: a way of speaking of Christian baptism.

5.31   The scripture: see Gen 2.24.

6.1   Some manuscripts omit it is your Christian duty to.

6.2-3   Commandment: see Deut 5.16.

6.12   Spiritual forces: see 1.21.
        The heavenly world: see 1.3.

6.17   The word of God: the Christian message.

6.19   the gospel's secret; some manuscripts have God's secret plan.

6.21   Tychicus: see Col 4.7.

<h2 style="text-align:center">PHILIPPIANS</h2>

1.1   Timothy: one of Paul's colleagues who traveled with him and
        helped in the work (see Acts 16.1-3).
        Philippi: a city in the Roman province of Macedonia, which
        corresponded to what is now northern Greece (see Acts 16.9-40).
        Church leaders: a translation of a word which means "overseers,"
        used of shepherds (see Acts 20.28; 1 Peter 2.25); the technical
        sense "bishops" hardly fits here.
        Helpers: a translation of a word which means "servants"; it may
        have the technical sense of "deacons" (see Rom 16.1; 1 Tim 3.8,12).

1.6   The Day: the final Day, when Christ will return as judge and
        king.

1.13   Palace guard: the soldiers stationed at the palace, either of
        the Roman governor in a city like Ephesus or Caesarea, or of the
        Emperor in Rome (see 4.22).

1.14   The message; some manuscripts have God's message.

2.1   You have fellowship with the Spirit; or The Spirit has brought
        you into fellowship with one another.

2.6   become; or remain.

2.9   The name: Lord (see verse 11).

2.10   The world below: the world of the dead.

2.15   You must shine; or You shine.

2.16   The Day of Christ: see 1.6.

2.19   Timothy: see 1.1.

2.20   He is the only one who shares my feelings and who; or There is no one else here like him, who.

2.25   Epaphroditus: the man who had brought to Paul the offering from the church in Philippi (see 4.18) and who now will return to Philippi with the letter.

3.2   Dogs: a contemptuous reference to those Jewish Christians who taught that Gentiles had to be circumcised (men who insist on cutting the body) in order to become Christians.

3.3   worship God by means of his Spirit; some manuscripts have worship God in our spirit; one manuscript has worship spiritually.

3.5   Pharisee: a member of a Jewish religious group which was strict in obeying the Law of Moses and other regulations which had been added to it through the centuries.

3.13   do not; some manuscripts have do not yet.

4.3   partner; or Syzygos (a man's name).

4.15   Macedonia: see note on 1.1.

4.16   Thessalonica: the capital city of the Roman province of Macedonia.

4.18   Epaphroditus: see 2.25.

4.22   Those who belong to the Emperor's palace: people in the service of the Roman Emperor, either in Rome or in the provincial capitals (see 1.13).

COLOSSIANS

1.1   Apostle: one who is commissioned to speak and act with the authority of the one who sent him.
        Timothy: one of Paul's colleagues who traveled with him and helped in the work (see Acts 16.1-3).

1.2   Colossae: a city in what was then the Roman province of Asia and is now western Turkey; Colossae was some 175 kilometers east of Ephesus, the capital of the province.
        God our Father; some manuscripts add and the Lord Jesus Christ.

1.7   Epaphras: the founder of the church at Colossae, who was now with Paul (4.12; see Philemon 23).
        our; some manuscripts have your.

1.11-12 with patience. And with joy give thanks to; or with patience and joy. And give thanks to.
        The kingdom of light: the kingdom of God, here spoken of as a future event.

made you fit; some manuscripts have made us fit.

1.15   He is the first-born Son, superior to all created things; or He was born before all things were created.

1.16   Spiritual powers, lords, rulers, and authorities: spiritual forces which control the universe.

1.21   You were far away from God: the Colossian Christians were Gentiles (see 2.13).

1.26   through all past ages from; or from all heavenly rulers and from.

1.27   The glory of God: all that God is and all that he will give to his people in the life to come.

2.1   Laodicea: a city about 17 kilometers west of Colossae.

2.2   God's secret, which is Christ himself; some manuscripts have God's secret; others have the secret of God the Father of Christ; others have the secret of the God and Father, and of Christ.

2.8   The ruling spirits of the universe: the evil spiritual forces which rule the world (also verse 20); or the Greek phrase may mean elementary and worthless religious rules (see Gal 4.3).

2.11   Circumcision: the Jewish rite which showed that the male child was a member of Israel, the people of God; the Christian rite of baptism portrays the same relation to God through Christ.

2.13   The Law: the Law of Moses, the revelation of God's will for his people Israel.

2.15   Christ freed himself from the power of the spiritual rulers and authorities; or Christ stripped the spiritual rulers and authorities of their power.
Spiritual rulers and authorities: see 1.16.
Captives in his victory procession: often a Roman general returning from a successful military campaign would parade with his troops through the streets of Rome, accompanied by his defeated enemies.

2.20   The ruling spirits of the universe: see 2.8.

2.23   but they have no real value in controlling physical passions; or they have no real value, but serve only to satisfy physical passions.

3.1   The right side: the place of honor and power (see Psa 110.1).

3.6   Some manuscripts omit upon those who do not obey him.

3.10   In his own image: see Gen 1.26-27.

3.14   all things; or all people.

3.15   The one body: the Church.

4.3   The secret of Christ: see 1.26,27; 2.2.

4.7   Tychicus: one of Paul's colleagues who helped him in the work; according to Acts 20.4 he was from the province of Asia (of which Ephesus was the capital); see also Eph 6.21; 2 Tim 4.12; Titus 3.12.

4.8   I am sending him: Tychicus would deliver to the Colossian Christians the letter that Paul had written them.

4.9   Onesimus: see Paul's letter to Philemon.

4.10   Aristarchus: one of Paul's colleagues, from Thessalonica (see Acts 19.29; 20.4; 27.2).
        Mark: John Mark, of Jerusalem (see Acts 12.12,25; 13.5,13; 15.37-39).
        Barnabas: an outstanding Christian leader, Paul's companion in the early years of his work (see Acts 4.36; 13.1--15.39).

4.12   Epaphras: see 1.7.

4.13   Laodicea: see 2.1.
        Hierapolis: a city about 20 kilometers northwest of Colossae.

4.14   Luke: according to ancient tradition Paul's companion on many of his travels.

4.15   Nympha...her house; some manuscripts have Nymphas...his house.

4.16   The letter that the brothers in Laodicea will send you: presumably a letter Paul has written (or intends to write) to the Christians in Laodicea; this letter has not been preserved unless it is, as some believe, what is now called the letter to the Ephesians.

4.17   Archippus: see Philemon 2.

1 THESSALONIANS

1.1   Silas: a colleague and assistant of Paul (see Acts 15.22--18.5).
        Timothy: see Col 1.1.
        Thessalonica: the capital city of the Roman province of Macedonia; for Paul's first visit there see Acts 17.1-9.

1.7   Macedonia: a Roman province which corresponded to what is now the northern half of Greece.

(103)

Achaia: a Roman province which corresponded to what is now the southern half of Greece; its capital city was Corinth, the place where Paul probably was when he wrote this letter.

2.2   Philippi: see Phil 1.1.
Before we came to you: see Acts 16.19-40.

2.7   we were gentle when we were with you, like a mother; some manuscripts have we were like children when we were with you; we were like a mother.

2.13   For God is at work; or For it is at work.

2.15   The prophets: either people who were God's messengers in Old Testament times or else Christian prophets (see Matt 23.29-37).

2.16   has at last come down; or has completely come down; or has come down forever.

2.18   Satan: the ruler of the forces of evil; the name means "the opponent."

3.1   Athens: a city in the province of Achaia; for Paul's stay there see Acts 17.15--18.1.

3.2   Timothy: see 1.1.
who works with us for God; or and God's fellow worker; some manuscripts have and God's servant.

3.6   Timothy has come back: see Acts 18.5.

3.13   all who belong to him; or all his angels.

4.4   live with his wife; or control his body.

4.10   Macedonia: see 1.7.

5.2   The Day of the Lord: the day of the Last Judgment.

2 THESSALONIANS

1.1   Silas and Timothy: see 1 Thes 1.1.
Thessalonica: see 1 Thes 1.1.

1.10   That Day: the day of the Last Judgment.

1.12   our God and of the Lord; or our God and Lord.

2.2   The Day of the Lord: see 1.10.

2.3   The final Rebellion...the Wicked One: a vague allusion to the
        expected increase of human sin and wickedness, whose human leader
        (see verse 9) will claim to be divine.
        God's Temple: probably the Temple in Jerusalem.

2.7   The one who holds it back: a vague allusion to some power,
        either of God or of Satan; it could be (see verse 6 something) the
        power of the Roman Empire.

2.13   as the first; some manuscripts have from the beginning.

3.3   The Evil One: the Devil (see Matt 6.13).

3.6   them; some manuscripts have you.

3.16   in every way; some manuscripts have in all places.

1 TIMOTHY

1.1   Apostle: one who is commissioned to speak and act with the
        authority of the one who sent him.

1.2   Timothy: see Col 1.1.

1.3   Ephesus: the capital city of the Roman province of Asia, in
        what is now western Turkey.
        Macedonia: a Roman province corresponding to what is now
        northern Greece.

1.4   Long lists of ancestors: probably lists of ancient Hebrew
        patriarchs, with comments on their activities.

1.8   The Law: the Law of Moses, the first five books of the Old
        Testament.

1.18   The words of prophecy: probably spoken by Christian prophets at
        Timothy's ordination to the Christian ministry (see 4.14).

1.20   Handing them over to the power of Satan: by being expelled from
        the Christian fellowship the two men were subject to Satan's
        destructive power (see 1 Cor 5.5).
        Blasphemy: speaking evil of God or of Christ.

2.15   will be saved through having children; or will be kept safe
        through childbirth.
        if she perseveres; or if they persevere.

3.1   This is a true saying; these words may belong at the end of the
        preceding verse (2.15).
        A church leader: the Greek word "overseer," "supervisor," which
        later acquired the technical sense of "bishop."

3.2   have only one wife; or be married only once; or be a faithful husband.

3.8   Church helpers: the Greek word "servants," which later acquired the technical sense of "deacons."

3.11   Their wives; or Women helpers.

3.12   have only one wife; or be married only once; or be a faithful husband.

3.16   He; some manuscripts have God.
        was shown to be right by the Spirit; or and, in spiritual form, was shown to be right.

4.5   The word of God: the divine command that brought all things into being.

4.9   struggle; some manuscripts have are reviled.

4.13   The Scriptures: the Hebrew Scriptures, the Old Testament.

4.14   The prophets: see 1.18.
        The elders: church officers whose precise duties are not specified (see Acts 11.30).

5.9   been married only once; or been a faithful wife.

5.12   Their earlier promise to him: the promise to dedicate them-selves exclusively to Christian service.

5.17   Elders...leaders: see 3.1; 4.14.

5.18   The scripture: see Deut 25.4.
        "A worker should be given his pay": see Luke 10.7; 1 Cor 9.14.

6.12   Before many witnesses: probably at the time of his ordination to Christian service (see 1.18; 4.14).

6.13   Pontius Pilate: the Roman governor of Judea (A.D. 26-36) who sentenced Jesus to death.

2 TIMOTHY

1.1   Apostle: see 1 Tim 1.1.

1.2   Timothy: see Col 1.1.

1.6   I laid my hands on you: a reference to Timothy's ordination to Christian service (see 1 Tim 1.18; 4.14).

1.12   That Day: the day of the Last Judgment.
what he has entrusted to me; or what I have entrusted to him.

1.15   Province of Asia: a Roman province in what is now western Turkey;
its capital city was Ephesus.

2.17   Hymenaeus: see 1 Tim 1.20.

2.26   who had caught them; or now that God has caught them.

3.8   Jannes and Jambres: according to Jewish tradition the names of
the Egyptian magicians who opposed Moses (see Exo 7.22; 9.11).

3.11   Antioch, Iconium, and Lystra: see Acts 13.14--14.20; 16.1-5.

3.15   The Holy Scriptures: the Hebrew Scriptures, the Old Testament.

3.16   All Scripture is inspired by God and is useful; or Every Scripture inspired by God is also useful.

4.7   kept the faith; or been true to my promise.

4.10   Demas: see Col 4.14.
Thessalonica: the capital of the Roman province of Macedonia.
Galatia; some manuscripts have Gaul.
Titus: see Gal 2.1.
Dalmatia: the southern half of the province of Illyricum, in
what is now Yugoslavia.

4.11   Luke: see Col 4.14.
Mark: see Col 4.10.

4.12   Tychicus: see Col. 4.7.

4.13   Troas: a city on the Aegean Sea, on what is now the western
coast of Turkey.

4.16   I defended myself: in a trial before the Roman authorities.

4.19   Priscilla and Aquila: see Acts 18.2-3,18-19.

4.20   Miletus: a prominent port city on the Aegean Sea, south of
Ephesus.

4.21   Winter: at which time travel by sea usually ceased.

TITUS

1.1   Apostle: see 1 Tim 1.1.

1.4   Titus: see Gal 2.1.

1.5   Crete: an island in the eastern Mediterranean.
Elders: see 1 Tim 4.14.

1.6   have only one wife; or be married only once; or be a faithful husband.

1.7   A church leader: see 1 Tim 3.1.

1.12-13   A Cretan himself: the Cretan poet Epimenides (6th century B.C.).

2.13   our great God and Savior Jesus Christ; or the great God and our Savior Jesus Christ.

3.1   to do good in every way; or for any kind of honest work.

3.5   through the Holy Spirit...washing us; or through the washing that brings new birth, the new life produced by the Holy Spirit.
Washing: a way of speaking about Christian baptism.

3.9   Long lists of ancestors: see 1 Tim 1.4.
The Law: the Law of Moses, the first five books of the Old Testament.

3.12   Tychicus: see Col 4.7.
Nicopolis: a town in the province of Achaia, on the shore of the Adriatic Sea.

3.13   Apollos: perhaps the same man spoken of in Acts 18.24--19.1; 1 Cor 3.1-9.

PHILEMON

1   Timothy: see Col 1.1.

2   Apphia: perhaps Philemon's wife.
Archippus: perhaps the son of Philemon and Apphia.

6   our fellowship with you; or your fellowship with us.

9   the ambassador of Christ Jesus, and at present also a prisoner for his sake; or an old man, and at present a prisoner for the sake of Christ Jesus.

11   Useful: Paul is making a play on words: the name Onesimus means "useful."

18   Done you any wrong: a runaway slave usually took with him money or valuables stolen from his master.

19   You owe your very self: probably meaning that Philemon had become a Christian as a result of Paul's preaching.

21   Do even more: perhaps a hint that Philemon should set Onesimus free.

23   Epaphras: see Col 1.7.

24   Mark: see Col 4.10.
        Luke: see Col 4.14.

HEBREWS

1.1   Our ancestors: the Hebrew people of the Old Testament.
        Prophets: God's messengers who proclaimed his message to the people of Israel.

1.2   These last days: the time of God's final revelation through Jesus Christ (see 9.26).

1.3   Glory: the visible manifestation of God's being.
        Right side: the place of honor and authority.

1.4   The name: that is, of Son, which none of the angels has.

1.5   God...said: see Psa 2.7 and 2 Sam 7.14.

1.6   He said: see Septuagint Deut 32.43; see Septuagint Psa 97.7.

1.7   God said: see Septuagint Psa 104.4.

1.8-9   God said: see Psa 45.6-7.

1.8   Your kingdom, O God, will last; or God is your kingdom.
        your; some manuscripts have his.

1.9   Honor: of being king.

1.10-12 He also said: see Septuagint Psa 102.25-27.

1.12   Some manuscripts omit like clothes.

1.13   God...said: see Psa 110.1.
        Right side: see 1.3.
        Footstool: a figure of defeat and humiliation.

2.2   Our ancestors: see 1.1.
        By the angels: according to popular Jewish teaching, angels were present when the Law was given to Moses at Mount Sinai (see Gal 3.19).

2.6   The Scriptures: see Psa 8.4-6.

2.7   For a little while: so the Septuagint of Psa 8.5 (Hebrew has
a little lower); here it refers to the time of Jesus' earthly life.
The angels: so the Septuagint of Psa 8.5; Hebrew has God.
Many manuscripts add: You made him ruler over everything you
made (see Psa 8.6).

2.10   Sons: those who become God's sons through the Son, Jesus Christ.

2.12   He says: see Psa 22.22.

2.13   He also says: see Septuagint Isa 8.17 and 8.18.

2.14   Devil: the ruler of the forces of evil; the name means "the
accuser."

2.16   The scripture: see Isa 41.8-9.

2.17   His brothers: those who have become God's sons (see verse 10).
   High Priest: in the Jewish religion the priest who occupied the
highest office; the title is given to Jesus as the one who repre-
sents his people before God and secures the forgiveness of their
sins.

3.1   High Priest: see 2.17.

3.2   God's house: probably a reference to the people of God, of whom
Moses was leader; Jesus, as God's Son (verse 6), is superior to
Moses, God's servant (verse 5; see Num 12.7).

3.6   in what we hope for; some manuscripts add firmly to the end
(see verse 14).

3.7-11   The Holy Spirit says: see Septuagint Psa 95.7-11.

3.8   That day in the desert: see Exo 17.1-7; Num 20.1-13.

3.15   The scripture: see Septuagint Psa 95.7-8.

3.19   The land: Canaan, the Promised Land.

4.2   when they heard it, they did not accept it with faith; some
manuscripts have they were not joined with those who heard it and
had faith.

4.3   He said: see Psa 95.11.

4.4   This is said: see Gen 2.2.

4.5   Is spoken of: see Psa 95.11.

4.7   The scripture: see Septuagint Psa 95.7-8.

4.14   High Priest: see 2.17.

5.4   Aaron: Moses' brother, the first High Priest (see Exo 28.1-2).

5.5   God said: see Psa 2.7.

5.6   He also said: see Psa 110.4.
        Melchizedek: see 7.1-19.

5.7   With loud cries and tears: in the Garden of Gethsemane (see
        Matt 26.36-46; Mark 14.32-42; Luke 22.41-43).

5.10   in the priestly order of Melchizedek; or like Melchizedek; or
        in the line of succession to Melchizedek.

5.12   Solid food...milk: figures of advanced teachings contrasted with
        elementary teachings; the readers' spiritual education had not
        progressed as it should have (see 6.1).

6.1   Useless works: actions by means of which a person hopes to gain
        God's favor.

6.2   baptisms; or purification ceremonies.
        The laying on of hands: it is not certain what specific rite
        this refers to.

6.4   Tasted: experienced.

6.7   The soil: a figure of those who respond to God's blessings; the
        soil that grows thorns and weeds (verse 8) is a figure of those
        whose lives and actions are not pleasing to God.

6.14   He said: see Gen 22.16-17.

6.18   These two things: God's promise and his vow to keep the promise.

6.19   The inner sanctuary: heaven is here compared to the Jewish
        Temple; a curtain separated the main sanctuary from the inner one,
        the Most Holy Place, where God's glory dwelt.

6.20   Jesus has gone in there: the Jewish High Priest entered the Most
        Holy Place once a year, to offer sacrifice for the people's sins;
        Jesus, as High Priest, has gone into the very presence of God, in
        heaven.

7.1   Melchizedek: see Gen 14.17-20.
        Salem: the city of Jerusalem.

7.5   Levi: one of the sons of Jacob, and head of the tribe from
        which all Hebrew priests were chosen.
        One tenth: the people of Israel gave one tenth of their income
        to pay for the cost of maintaining the priesthood (see Num 18.21).

7.8   As the scripture says: the biblical account says nothing of Melchizedek's death.

7.17   The scripture: see Psa 110.4.
        in the priestly order of Melchizedek; or like Melchizedek; or: in the line of succession to Melchizedek.

7.21   God said: see Psa 110.4.

7.22   Covenant: an agreement or pact; here it refers to God's covenant with his people (see 8.6).

7.26   High Priest: see 2.17.
        Above the heavens: into the very presence of God.

8.1   The right: the place of honor and authority.
        The Divine Majesty: a title of God.

8.5   God said: see Exo 25.40.

8.7   The first covenant: the one given at Mt. Sinai.

8.8-12 He says: see Septuagint Jer 38.31-34.

9.11   High Priest: see 2.17.
        are already here; some manuscripts have are coming or were coming.

9.12   Most Holy Place: in heaven, into the very presence of God (see 6.20).

9.14   the eternal Spirit; or his eternal spirit.
        our...we; some manuscripts have your...you.

9.18   Covenant: in Greek the same word means "will" (verses 16-17) and "covenant."

9.19   Some manuscripts omit and goats.
        The book of the Law: the record of God's laws for the people of Israel (see Exo 24.6-8).
        Hyssop: a small bushy plant which was used in ceremonies of sprinkling.

9.20   He said: see Exo 24.8.

9.28   A second time: the final coming at the end of the age.

10.5-7 He said: see Septuagint Psa 40.6-8.

10.7   The book of the Law: see 9.19.

10.9   So God...the sacrifice of Christ; or So Christ...his own sacrifice.

10.12   Right side: the place of honor and authority.

10.13   Footstool: see 1.13.

10.15-16 He says: see Jer 31.33.

10.17   He says: see Jer 31.34.

10.25   The Day of the Lord: the Last Judgment.

10.30   Who said: see Deut 32.35.
Who also said: see Deut 32.36.

10.37-38 The scripture says: see Septuagint Hab 2.3-4.

10.38   my righteous people...if any of them; or my righteous servant
...if he.

11.4   Abel: see Gen 4.3-10.

11.5   Enoch: see Septuagint Gen 5.21-24.

11.7   Noah: see Gen 6.13-22.

11.8   Abraham: see Gen 12.1-5.

11.11   Abraham: see Gen 18.11-14; 21.2.
It was faith...children. He; some manuscripts have It was faith
that made Sarah herself able to conceive, even though she was too
old to have children. She.

11.17   Abraham: see Gen 22.1-14.

11.18   God had said: see Gen 21.12.

11.20   Isaac: see Gen 27.27-29,39-40.

11.21   Jacob: see Gen 48.1-20.
The top of his walking stick: see Septuagint Gen 47.31.

11.22   Joseph: see Gen 50.24-25.

11.23   The parents of Moses: see Exo 2.2.

11.24   Moses: see Exo 2.10-12.

11.28   The Passover: see Exo 12.21-28.

11.29   The Israelites: see Exo 14.21-31.

11.30   Jericho: see Josh 6.12-21.

11.31   Rahab: see Josh 2.1-21; 6.22-25.

(113)

11.37   they were sawn in two; <u>some manuscripts add</u> they were put on trial.

12.1   <u>Witnesses</u>: not spectators, but those who gave their testimony of <u>faith</u> (chapter 11).

12.2   because of the joy; <u>or</u> in place of the joy.
<u>The right side</u>: the place of honor and authority.

12.5-6   <u>God speaks</u>: see Septuagint Prov 3.11-12.

12.16   <u>Esau</u>: see Gen 25.29-34; 27.30-40.

12.17   <u>Receive his father's blessing</u>: see Gen 27.30-40.
<u>change what he had done</u>; <u>or</u> change his father's mind.
<u>he looked for it</u>; <u>or</u> he tried to get the blessing.

12.18-19   <u>Mount Sinai</u>: see Exo 19.16-22; 20.18-21.

12.21   <u>Moses said</u>: see Deut 9.19.

12.22   <u>Mount Zion</u>: here a figure of the heavenly sanctuary of God.

12.26   <u>He has promised</u>: see Septuagint Hag 2.6.

13.2   <u>Welcomed angels</u>: see Gen 18.1-8; 19.1-3.

13.5   <u>God has said</u>: see Deut 31.6.

13.6   <u>And say</u>: see Septuagint Psa 118.6.

13.12   <u>The city</u>: Jerusalem.

13.21   us; <u>some manuscripts have</u> you.

13.23   <u>Timothy</u>: a Christian leader who was a colleague and assistant of the apostle Paul (see Acts 16.1-3).

13.25   from Italy; <u>or</u> in Italy.

JAMES

1.13   cannot be tempted by evil; <u>or</u> has nothing to do with evil.

1.18   <u>Brought us into being</u>: here not physical creation but the spiritual birth effected by God.

2.7   <u>That good name</u>: the name of Christian.

2.8   <u>The scripture</u>: see Lev 19.18.

2.11   <u>Who said</u>: see Exo 20.13,14.

2.20   useless; <u>some manuscripts have</u> dead.

2.21   <u>Abraham</u>: see Gen 22.1-14.

2.23   <u>The scripture</u>: see Septuagint Gen 15.6.
<u>God's friend</u>: see Isa 41.8.

2.25   <u>Rahab</u>: see Josh 2.1-21.

3.6   the entire course of our existence; <u>or</u> the whole realm of nature.

4.5   <u>The scripture</u>: the source of this quotation is unknown.
<u>The spirit...desires</u>; <u>or</u> God yearns jealously over the spirit
that he placed in us.

4.6   <u>The scripture</u>: see Septuagint Prov 3.34.

4.7   <u>Devil</u>: the ruler of the forces of evil; the name means "the
accuser."

4.14   what your life tomorrow will be!; <u>or</u> what tomorrow will be like.
What is your life?

5.6   people, and they do not resist you; <u>or</u> people. Will God not
resist you?

5.11   <u>Job</u>: see Job 2.10; 42.10.

5.14   <u>Elders</u>: church officers whose precise duties are not specified
(see Acts 11.30).
<u>Olive oil</u>: for its use as a medicine see Mark 6.13; Luke 10.34.

5.17-18 <u>Elijah</u>: see 1 Kgs 17.1; 18.42-45.

5.20   that sinner's soul; <u>or</u> his own soul.

1 PETER

1.2   <u>The provinces</u>: all five Roman provinces named were in what is
now the country of Turkey.

1.6   <u>Be glad</u>; <u>or</u> You are glad.

1.7   <u>The Day</u>: of the Last Judgment.

1.8   seen; <u>some manuscripts have</u> known.

1.10   <u>The prophets</u>: God's messengers who proclaimed his message to
the people of Israel.

1.11   when the time would be and how it would come; <u>or</u> who the person
would be and when he would come.

1.16 The scripture: see Lev 19.2.

1.22 with all your heart; some manuscripts have with a pure heart.

1.23 the living and eternal word of God; or the word of the living and eternal God.

1.24 The scripture: see Septuagint Isa 40.6-8.

2.3 The scripture: see Psa 34.8.

2.6 The scripture: see Septuagint Isa 28.16.
Zion: probably a reference to the Temple; it could be the city of Jerusalem.

2.7 The stone: see Psa 118.22.

2.8 Another scripture: see Isa 8.14.

2.13 Emperor: of the Roman Empire.

2.14 Governors: of the Roman provinces.

2.21 suffered; some manuscripts have died.

2.24 to the cross; or on the cross.

3.6 Sarah: see Gen 18.12.

3.10-12 The scripture: see Septuagint Psa 34.12-16.

3.18 died; many manuscripts have suffered.
you; some manuscripts have us.

3.19 Preached: either the Good News of salvation (see 4.6) or God's punishment on them.
Imprisoned: in Sheol, the world of the dead.

3.20 Those who had not obeyed God: probably the contemporaries of Noah who did not follow Noah's example; less likely, the rebel angels (see 2 Peter 2.4).
Noah: see Gen 6.1--7.24.
Eight: Noah and his wife and their three sons and their wives.
were saved by the water; or were brought safely through the water.

3.22 Right side: the place of honor and authority.

4.6 The dead: see 3.19.

4.11 Serves: perhaps in the technical sense of "serves as a deacon" (see 1 Tim 3.8).

4.12   Painful test: persecution for being Christians.

4.14   glorious; some manuscripts add and mighty.

4.18   The scripture: see Septuagint Prov 11.31.

5.1   Elder: a church officer whose precise duties are not specified (see Acts 11.30).

5.2   Some manuscripts omit and to take care of it; others omit as God wants you to.

5.4   Chief Shepherd: Jesus Christ.

5.5   The scripture: see Septuagint Prov 3.34.

5.8   Devil: the ruler of the forces of evil; the name means "the accuser."

5.12   Silas: probably the same man who was a colleague and assistant of Paul (see Acts 15.22--18.5).

5.13   Babylon: as in the book of Revelation (see chapter 18), this probably refers to Rome.
Mark: perhaps John Mark, of Jerusalem (see Col 4.10); if so, son here means "follower, assistant."

2 PETER

1.1   of our God and Savior Jesus Christ; or of our God and of our Savior Jesus Christ.

1.3   to share in his own; some manuscripts have through his.

1.10   abandon your faith; or fall into sin.

1.17   There: at the transfiguration of Jesus (see Matt 17.1-8; Mark 9.2-8; Luke 9.28-36).
The Supreme Glory: a title of God.
This is my own dear Son, with whom I am pleased: these words reflect such Old Testament passages as Psa 2.7; Gen 22.2; Deut 18.15.
my own dear Son; or my only Son; or my Son, the Beloved.

1.19   Prophets: God's messengers who proclaimed his message to the people of Israel.

1.21   men; some manuscripts have holy men.

2.1   False prophets: people who falsely claimed they had a message from God.

2.3   Their judge...their Destroyer: God.

2.4   Hell: a translation of the Greek "Tartarus," which in Greek mythology was the place of punishment for the rebel gods.
       chained in darkness; some manuscripts have in dark pits.

2.5   The flood: see Gen 6.1--7.24.

2.6   Sodom and Gomorrah: see Gen 19.24-25.

2.7   Lot: see Gen 19.1-16,29.

2.10   The glorious beings above: angelic powers (see Jude 8).

2.13   deceitful ways; some manuscripts have fellowship meals (see Jude 12).

2.15   Balaam: see Num 22.4-35.

2.22   A dog: see Prov 26.11.

3.2   Prophets: see 1.19.

3.4   He: Christ.

3.10   vanish; some manuscripts have be found; others have be burned up; one has be found destroyed.

1 JOHN

1.4   our; some manuscripts have your.

1.5   Light: a biblical figure for life and truth.
       Darkness: a biblical figure for death and falsehood.

2.1   My children: an intimate term of address, implying perhaps that the writer is an old man (see also verses 12,14,18,28).

2.10   in him...someone else; or in it...him.

2.13   Him who has existed from the beginning: Jesus Christ.
       The Evil One: the Devil, the ruler of the forces of evil.

2.18   The Enemy of Christ: the leader of the forces of evil who in the end will oppose Christ.

2.20   all of you know the truth; some manuscripts have you know everything.

2.25   us; some manuscripts have you.

3.2   when Christ appears; or when it is made clear.

3.5   sins; <u>some manuscripts have</u> our sins.

3.7   <u>My children</u>: see 2.1.

3.8   <u>The Devil</u>: the ruler of the forces of evil; the name means "the accuser."

3.12 <u>Cain</u>: see Gen 4.3-8.
      <u>The Evil One</u>: see 2.13.

3.19 <u>This</u>: the reality and practice of Christian love (verses 16-18).

3.23 <u>As Christ commanded</u>: see John 13.34; 15.12,17.

4.1   <u>False prophets</u>: people who falsely claimed they had a message from God.

4.3   <u>The Enemy of Christ</u>: see 2.18.

4.6   <u>We belong to God</u>: the writer and his fellow teachers of Christian truth, in contrast with the false prophets (verse 5).

5.18 <u>The Evil One</u>: see 2.13.

5.21 <u>My children</u>: see 2.1.

2 JOHN

1   <u>The Elder</u>: probably an official church title, not simply a designation of the writer as an old man.

2   <u>Lady and...her children</u>: this probably refers to a church and its members (also in verses 4-5).
     dear Lady; <u>or</u> Lady chosen by God.

7   <u>The Enemy of Christ</u>: see 1 John 2.18.

8   we; <u>some manuscripts have</u> you.

9   the teaching of Christ; <u>or</u> the teaching about Christ.

13   <u>Children of your dear Sister</u>: this probably refers to the members of the church to which the writer belonged.
     dear Sister; <u>or</u> Sister chosen by God.

3 JOHN

1   <u>The Elder</u>: see 2 John 1.

4   <u>My children</u>: see 1 John 2.1.

9   The church: probably the church to which Gaius belongs.

12   Demetrius: perhaps the one who took the letter to Gaius.

JUDE

1   James: perhaps the leader of the church in Jerusalem (see Acts
15.13; Gal 1.19).

4   Jesus Christ, our only Master and Lord; or our only Master and
our Lord Jesus Christ.

5   the Lord; some manuscripts have Jesus, which in Greek is the
same as Joshua.
         Rescued...destroyed: see Exo 12.51; Num 14.26-38.

7   Sodom and Gomorrah: see Gen 19.1-24.

8   The glorious beings above: angelic powers.

9   Michael: according to Jewish teaching Michael, who was one of
the chief angels, and the Devil each claimed the right to dispose
of Moses' body.

11   Cain: see Gen 4.3-8.
         Balaam: see Num 22.1-35.
         Korah: see Num 16.1-35.

12   dirty spots; or hidden dangers.
         Fellowship meals: special meals which the Christians ate to-
gether, ending with a celebration of the Lord's Supper (see
1 Cor 11.20-21).

14   Enoch...prophesied: this quotation is from "The Book of Enoch,"
a Jewish work of that time which was read by Jews and Christians.

17   Apostles: originally the twelve men chosen by Jesus as his
followers and messengers; later the title was given to others who,
like Paul, had not been followers of Jesus during his lifetime.

REVELATION

1.3   One who reads...those who listen: a reference to the public
reading of the book in church service.

1.4   Asia: a Roman province in what is now western Turkey; the
seven churches are named in verse 11.

1.9   Patmos: a small island in the Aegean Sea, some 100 kilometers
southwest of Ephesus, used by the Romans as a penal colony.

1.10   The Lord's day: Sunday.

1.13   What looked like a human being: see Dan 7.13.

1.18   World of the dead: it was thought of as a vast abyss in the depths of the earth.

1.20   Angels: either the guardians or the representatives of the seven churches.

2.6   Nicolaitans: a group which was apparently guilty of idolatry and immorality (see verse 15); it is probable that they are referred to also in verses 14,20,24.

2.7   Tree of life: see Gen 2.9.

2.9   Claim to be Jews: these really were not part of the people of God, as they claimed.
        Satan: a name of the Devil, the ruler of the forces of evil; the name means "the opponent."

2.10   Ten days: a figure for a relatively short time.

2.11   The second death: eternal, spiritual death (see 20.14; 21.8).

2.13   Where Satan has his throne: the city of Pergamum is condemned as being under the domination of evil; it was famous as a center of emperor worship.

2.14   Balaam...Balak: see Num 22-24; 31.16; Deut 23.4.

2.15   Nicolaitans: see 2.6.

2.17   Manna: the food that God provided for the Israelites during their wanderings in the wilderness after leaving Egypt (see Exo 16.14-15,31-35).

2.20   that woman; some manuscripts have your wife.
        Jezebel: probably a symbolic name for a woman who was like the wicked idolatrous wife of King Ahab of Israel (see 1 Kgs 16.30-31; 2 Kgs 9.22).

2.24   Deep secrets of Satan: secret teachings which were taught only to those who belonged to the heretical group (see 2.6).

2.28   The morning star: a figure of Christ himself (see 22.16).

3.4   White: a symbol of victory and joy.

3.5   Book of the living: the list kept by God of the names of all his people (see 13.8; 20.12,15).

3.7   The key that belonged to David: a symbol of the authority of the Messiah, who is a descendant of King David, to whom God promised a successor who would rule over God's people (see Isa 22.22; Acts 2.20-31).

3.9   Claim that they are Jews: see 2.9.

3.14   The Amen: Christ is the guarantee that God will keep all the promises he has made to his people (see 2 Cor 1.20).
        origin; or ruler.

4.3   Jasper: of varying colors; here probably green.
        Carnelian: usually red.
        Emerald: green.

4.4   Twenty-four elders: probably the heavenly representatives of the people of God in Old Testament times (the twelve tribes of Israel) and in New Testament times (the twelve apostles of Christ).

4.7   a face like a man's face; some manuscripts have a man's face.

5.3   The world below: the world of the dead (see 1.18).

5.5   The Lion...the great descendant of David: Jesus Christ.

6.6   A day's wages: this price for a quart of wheat and for three quarts of barley is very high and indicates scarcity of grain.

6.8   Hades: the world of the dead (see 1.18).

6.9   The altar: see 2.3.

7.2   Seal: an instrument used for marking objects or people with the symbol or name of their owner (see verse 3).

9.1   Star: here a figure of an angel (see verse 11).
        Abyss: the place in the depths of the earth where the demons were imprisoned until their final punishment.

9.3   Scorpion: a small creature with eight legs and a long tail with a poisonous sting; it can inflict a very painful, and sometimes fatal, wound.

9.4   God's seal: see 7.3.

9.14   Euphrates River: at that time it marked the eastern border of the Roman Empire.

9.20   What they themselves had made: idols which they worshiped.

11.2   The Holy City: Jerusalem.
        Forty-two months: the same as 1,260 days (verse 3); this period of time (three and a half years) was symbolic of a time of persecution and suffering.

11.7   The beast...of the abyss: see 13.1-7.

11.8   The great city: Jerusalem.
        Sodom: see Isa 1.10.

11.12   The two prophets: the two witnesses (verse 3).

11.19   Covenant Box: the symbol of God's covenant with his people; the
        Covenant Box of the Israelites was in the Most Holy Place in the
        Temple (see 1 Kgs 8.1-6).

12.3   Dragon: an imaginary beast thought to be like a huge lizard;
        here it appears as a figure of the Devil.

12.7   Michael: one of the chief angels.

12.14   Three and a half years: the same as 1,260 days (verse 6).

12.18   And the dragon stood; some manuscripts have And I stood,
        connecting this verse with what follows.

13.2   The dragon: see 12.3.

13.5   Forty-two months: see 11.2.

13.7   Some manuscripts omit It was allowed to fight against God's
        people and to defeat them.

13.8   The book of the living: see 3.5.
        whose names...was killed; or whose names were written in the
        book of the living which belongs to the Lamb that was killed
        before the creation of the world.

13.10   is meant to be killed by the sword; some manuscripts have kills
        with the sword.

13.18   The number stands for a man's name: both in Greek and Hebrew
        numbers were indicated by letters of the alphabet; the sum of the
        letters in various Hebrew and Greek names adds up to 666.
        666; some manuscripts have 616.

14.1   Mount Zion: Jerusalem.

14.4   Kept themselves pure...virgins: a figure of complete devotion
        to God and abstention from all idol worship.

14.8   Babylon: a name for Rome.

14.10   Sulfur: a yellow substance which burns with great heat and
        produces an unpleasant smell.

15.2   Name...number: see 13.18.

15.3   The song of Moses: see Exo 15.1-18.
nations; some manuscripts have ages.

16.12   Euphrates River: see 9.14.
The east: the region then known as Parthia.

16.16   Armageddon: "Hill of Megiddo" in northern Palestine, where the Israelites had fought crucial battles (see 2 Kgs 23.29-30).

16.19   Babylon: see 14.8.

17.1   That great city: Rome, which in Revelation is called Babylon (see 14.8).

17.8   That beast...from the abyss: see 11.7.
The book of the living: see 3.5.

18.3   have drunk her wine; some manuscripts have have been destroyed by her wine.

18.20   These words are probably spoken by the angel (verse 1) or else come from the author of the book.

18.24   These words are probably the author's comment, giving the reason why Babylon is to be destroyed.

19.4   Amen: a Hebrew word meaning "It is so" or "So be it."

19.10   the truth that Jesus revealed; or the Christian message about Jesus.

19.13   covered; some manuscripts have spattered.

19.19   The beast: the first beast, that came up out of the sea (13.1-10).

19.20   The false prophet: the second beast, that came up out of the earth (13.11-15).
The lake of fire: hell, or Gehenna (see 14.10; 20.10).
Sulfur: see 14.10.

20.1   The abyss: see 9.1.

20.4   The mark of the beast: see 13.16; 14.9.

20.6   The second death: see 20.14; 21.8.

20.8   Gog and Magog: symbolic names for the nations assembled against God's people; for the names see Ezek 38 and 39.

20.9   The city that he loves: Jerusalem.
from heaven; some manuscripts have out of heaven from God.

20.12   The book of the living: see 3.5.

20.13   <u>The world of the dead</u>: see 1.18.

21.3   <u>Some manuscripts omit</u> and he will be their God.

21.11   <u>Jasper</u>: see 4.3.

21.16-17   <u>Fifteen hundred miles long...216 feet high</u>: the Greek text speaks of "12,000 furlongs" and "144 cubits," which may have symbolic significance.

21.17   high; <u>or</u> thick.

21.19   <u>Sapphire</u>: usually blue.
<u>Agate</u>: of varying colors.
<u>Emerald</u>: green.

21.20   <u>Onyx</u>: of varying colors.
<u>Carnelian</u>: usually red.
<u>Beryl</u>: usually green or bluish-green.
<u>Topaz</u>: usually yellow.
<u>Chalcedony</u>: usually milky or gray.
<u>Turquoise</u>: blue or bluish-green.
<u>Amethyst</u>: usually purple or violet.

21.27   <u>Book of the living</u>: see 3.5.

22.14   wash their robes clean; <u>some manuscripts have</u> obey his commandments.
<u>The tree of life</u>: see 2.7.

22.21   everyone; <u>some manuscripts have</u> God's people; <u>others have</u> all of God's people.
<u>Some manuscripts add</u> Amen.